From an objective standpoint, the Cube of Sensation
is composed of:
Ideas = lines
Images (internal) = planes
Images of objects = solids

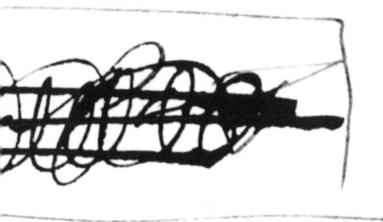

Essay on Poetry

Fernando Pessoa

Writings on Art and Poetical Theory

Fernando Pessoa

Writings on Art and Poetical Theory

Edited, with Notes and an Introduction
by Nuno Ribeiro & Cláudia Souza

Contra Mundum Press   New York · London · Melbourne

Writings on Art & Poetical Theory © 2021 Nuno Ribeiro & Cláudia Souza.

First Contra Mundum Press Edition 2021.

Library of Congress Cataloguing-in-Publication Data

Pessoa, Fernando, 1888–1935

[Writings on Art & Poetical Theory. English.]

Writings on Art & Poetical Theory / Fernando Pessoa; Edited by Nuno Ribeiro & Cláudia Souza

—1st Contra Mundum Press Edition

240 pp., 5 × 8 in.

ISBN 9781940625508

    I. Pessoa, Fernando.
   II. Title.
  III. Ribeiro, Nuno, & Souza, Cláudia
  IV. Editors.

2021944160

Table of Contents

Introduction

NUNO RIBEIRO *&* CLÁUDIA SOUZA

1 ☞ Pessoa's Education in Durban and His English Writings

Writings on Art and Poetical Theory contains a selection of Fernando Pessoa's writings (1888–1935) on art and poetical theory, originally written in English. In Pessoa's work one finds not only literary and fictional works but also a multiplicity of theoretical texts on the most diverse subjects concerning artistic movements, literature, and writers. One of the most important dimensions of Pessoa's writing corresponds to his critical and essayistic texts. Throughout his life, Pessoa published a series of critical and theoretical writings — mostly in Portuguese[1] — that were important for the establishment of modernism in Portugal. In addition to his Portuguese writings, the Pessoa Archive also contains a series of English texts on literary criticism that he left unpublished but intended to publish abroad.

Pessoa's English texts are the result in part of his education. Pessoa spent most of his childhood and adolescence in Durban, South Africa, where he lived between 1896 and 1905 and received an English education, following the marriage of his mother, Maria Madalena

1. An exception to this is a juvenile work about "Macaulay," published in *The Durban High School Magazine*, in December 1904. For further information about this, see: Pauly Ellen Bothe, *Apreciações Literárias de Fernando Pessoa* (Lisbon: Imprensa Nacional — Casa da Mœda, 2013) 169–174.

Pinheiro Nogueira, to Pessoa's stepfather, João Miguel Rosa, who was a Portuguese consul in Durban. The importance of Pessoa's English education is highlighted by Hubert D. Jennings in the book *Fernando Pessoa: The Poet with Many Faces*:

> It was an *"exutoire providentiel,"* as Armand Guibert describes it, which took Fernando Pessoa to South Africa. On January 6, 1896, he and his mother left Lisbon for Durban, where he was to spend the next ten years of his life. The experience, and particularly the English education he received there, was to transform his life, permeate his work, and leave a marked influence upon the literary trends of modern Portugal.[2]

In Durban, Pessoa first studies in the Convent School of Saint Joseph's (1896–1899) and is transferred in 1899 to Durban High School, where he is a peer of "young graduates from Oxford or Cambridge."[3] During this period, Pessoa reads the most diverse authors of the English literary tradition, who would become an everlasting presence in his work. In a letter written in 1932 to José Osório de Oliveira, Pessoa — referring to the books &

2. See the chapter "Fernando Pessoa in South Africa" in Hubert D. Jennings, Fernando Pessoa: *The Poet with Many Faces*, ed. Carlos Pitella (Lisbon: Tinta-da-China, 2019) 31.

3. *Ibid.*, 43.

authors that most influenced him — provides us with a relevant testimony of how important English literature was to him during his formative period in South Africa:

> In my childhood & early adolescence there was for me, who lived and was educated in English lands, a supreme and engaging book — Dickens' *Pickwick Papers*; even today, & for that reason, I read and reread it as if I did nothing more than remember.
>
> In my second adolescence, Shakespeare and Milton dominated my spirit, as well as, incidentally, those English romantic poets who are irregular shadows of them; among these, Shelley was perhaps the one whose inspiration I most lived with.
>
> In what I can call my third adolescence, spent here in Lisbon, I lived in the atmosphere of the Greek and German philosophers, as well as that of the decadent French, whose action was suddenly swept from my mind by Swedish gymnastics and by reading *Dégénérescence*, by Nordau.[4]

4. Fernando Pessoa, *Correspondência: 1923–1935*, ed. Manuela Parreira da Silva (Lisbon: Assírio & Alvim, 1999) 278–279. The translations from Portuguese are our own whenever we quote an original Portuguese edition, except in the cases we've been able to identify an English translation. In the latter case, we quote from existing translations.

In a document entitled "Influências" ["Influences"], Pessoa provides a detailed account of other poets who were important to him during his stay in South Africa:

> 1904–1905 — Influences of Milton and the English poets of the romantic period — Byron, Shelley, Keats & Tennyson. (Also, a little later, and influencing initially the *short story writer*, Edgar Poe.) Slight influences also from Pope's school. In prose, Carlyle. Remains of influences of Portuguese sub-poets read in childhood. — In this period the order of influences was, more or less: 1) Byron; 2) Milton, Pope and Byron; 3) Byron, Milton, Pope, Keats, Tennyson and Shelley somewhat; 4) Milton, Keats, Tennyson, Wordsworth & Shelley; 5) Shelley, Wordsworth, Keats and Poe.[5]

Both the letter sent to Oliveira and the document entitled "Influências" present just some of the English poets read by Pessoa in Durban. Throughout his Private Library and the documents present in the Pessoa Archive there are several other clues that enable us to understand the impact of English literature on Pessoa goes

---

5. Fernando Pessoa, *Escritos Autobiográficos, Automáticos e de Reflexão Pessoal*, ed. Richard Zenith (Lisbon: Assírio & Alvim, 2003) 150.

beyond the names referenced in those two texts. Indeed, throughout his life, Pessoa never abandons the English language. The Portuguese author works, in Lisbon, as a translator of English (and French) commercial letters. He also publishes translations into Portuguese of English-speaking poets such as Wordsworth, Coleridge, Shelley, Elizabeth & Robert Browning, and Poe.[6] That the Pessoa Archive contains thousands of pages written by Pessoa originally in English testifies to his continued engagement with English literature. The aforementioned evidence enables us to understand the impact of Pessoa's English education not only on his work but also on his life.

2 ☞ The Plural Literary Space and the Writings on Art and Poetical Theory

Pessoa's writings on art and poetical theory must be considered in the context of the development of a plural literary space. In a random note written by Pessoa one reads: "Be plural like the universe!"[7] This is precisely what he tries to achieve with his work through the

6. For further information regarding Pessoa's translations, see: Arnaldo Saraiva, *Fernando Pessoa Poeta — Tradutor de Poetas* (Porto: Lello Editores 1996).

7. Fernando Pessoa, *The Selected Prose of Fernando Pessoa*, ed. & tr. by Richard Zenith (New York: Grove Press, 2001) 237.

creation of a multiplicity of literary fictional authors[8] entrusted with the task of signing different texts and assuming a plurality of literary tasks, which is what one finds underlying Pessoa's heteronymic theory.

The concept of the heteronym as created by Pessoa is different from a simple pseudonym. In a "Bibliographical Summary" published in the literary journal *Presença* (December 1928), one reads:

> Fernando Pessoa's writings belong to two categories of works, which we may call orthonymic and heteronymic. We cannot call them autonymous and pseudonymous, for that's not in fact what they are. Pseudonymous works are by the author in his own person, except in the name he signs; heteronymic works are by the author outside his own person. They proceed from a full-fledged individual created by him, like the lines spoken by a character in a drama he might write.
>
> The heteronymic works of Fernando Pessoa have been produced by (so far) three people's names — Alberto Caeiro, Ricardo Reis, and Álvaro de Campos. These individuals should be considered distinct from their author.[9]

8. For further information regarding the term "fictional authors" to characterize Pessoa's creation of literary personalities, see: Fernando Pessoa, *Eu sou uma antologia: 136 autores fictícios*, Jerónimo Pizarro and Patricio Ferrari (eds) (Lisbon: Tinta-da-

According to this text, the writings of Pessoa can be distinguished by two categories: the orthonymic, signed by Pessoa in his own name, and the heteronymic, signed by literary fictional authors created by that author. The heteronymic works are different from the merely pseudonymous works, since the latter are written by the author in his own person, that is, with the simple shift of name, while the heteronymic works are written by each individual author and are distinct from his own persona. Thus, the creation of a heteronym corresponds to the creation of a different literary fictional author with its own writings, its own biography, its own way of seeing the world, and its own style, that is, as if the works a heteronym produces were written by a completely different person. In the text entitled *Aspects*, which was supposed to serve as an introduction to the publication of the works of the heteronyms, one reads:

> Each of the more enduring personalities,
> lived by the author within himself, was given
> an expressive nature and made the author of
> one or more books whose ideas, emotions,

← China: 2013). Following this edition, we employ the term "fictional author" as a general one that encompasses all the different types of fictional personalities created by Pessoa: heteronyms, semi-heteronyms, and literary personalities.

9. Fernando Pessoa, *A Little Larger Than the Entire Universe*, ed. and tr. by Richard Zenith (New York: Penguin Books, 2006) 3.

and literary art have no relationship to the real author (or perhaps only apparent author, since we don't know what reality is) except insofar as he served, when he wrote them, as the medium of the characters he created.

Neither this work nor those to follow have anything to do with the man who writes them. He doesn't agree or disagree with what's in them. He writes as if he were being dictated to. And as if the person dictating were a friend (and for that reason could freely ask him to write down what he dictates), the writer finds the dictation interesting, perhaps just out of friendship.[10]

As asserted in the "Bibliographical Summary," the only fictional authors Pessoa considers having achieved the status of a heteronym correspond to the name of three of his literary creations: Alberto Caeiro, Ricardo Reis, & Álvaro de Campos. Besides these heteronyms, Pessoa attributes the name of the semi-heteronym to Bernardo Soares, a fictional author entrusted with the task of signing Pessoa's *The Book of Disquiet* at its final stage.[11]

10. Fernando Pessoa, *The Selected Prose of Fernando Pessoa*, op. cit., 2.

11. Pessoa's *The Book of Disquiet* has three distinct stages: 1st) between 1913 & 1914, corresponding to a period when this project is signed by Pessoa in his own name; 2nd) between 1915 & 1920, when Vicente Guedes assumes the authorship of this project; 3rd) the final stage, when the project becomes the property of Bernardo

In a letter — written January 13, 1935, sent to Adolfo Casais Monteiro — known as the letter on the genesis of the heteronyms, one reads the following description of Bernardo Soares as a semi-heteronym:

> My semiheteronym Bernardo Soares, who in many ways resembles Álvaro de Campos, always appears when I'm sleepy or drowsy, such that my qualities of inhibition and logical reasoning are suspended; his prose is an endless reverie. He's a semiheteronym because his personality, although not my own, doesn't differ from my own but is a mere mutilation of it. He's me without my logical reasoning and emotion. His prose is the same as mine, except for a certain formal restraint that reason imposes on my own writing, and his Portuguese is exactly the same — whereas Caeiro writes bad Portuguese, Campos writes it reasonably well but with mistakes

← Soares — between 1929 & 1935, after a period of silence regarding that project (between 1921 and 1928, Pessoa doesn't write any fragments for *The Book of Disquiet*). For further information regarding this, see: Nuno Ribeiro, "Poéticas do Inacabado — Pessoa, Wittgenstein e o Livro por Vir," in: Osmar Pereira Oliva (org.), *Literatura, Vazio e Danação* (Montes Claros: Editora Unimontes, 2013) 223–241; Nuno Ribeiro, "Wittgenstein and Pessoa: The Archive as 'Open Work' in Eco's Perspective," in Pamela Arancibia et al., *Philological Concerns: Textual Criticism Throughout the Centuries* (Firenze: Franco Cesati Editore, 2016) 207–221.

> such as "me myself" instead of "I myself," etc.,
> and Reis writes better than I, but with a pur-
> ism I find excessive. What's hard for me is to
> write the prose of Reis — still unpublished —
> or of Campos. Simulation is easier, because
> more spontaneous, in verse.[12]

According to this excerpt, the difference between the heteronym and the semi-heteronym corresponds to the manner of writing, that is, the style. Whereas the heteronym is different from its creator in his style, the semi-heteronym is only different in his way of thinking & perceiving the world, but with the same style of writing as his creator, for Pessoa explicitly says that, though Bernardo Soares is a *mutilation* of the Portuguese author's personality ("He's me without my logical reasoning and emotion"), his prose style is the same as his.

Nevertheless, Pessoa's creation of literary fictional authors doesn't come to an end with the creation of the heteronymic and semi-heteronymic works. In the Pessoa Archive one finds a multiplicity of other personalities created during the same period. Though there is considerable debate in Pessoa studies about how to name them — Pessoa himself doesn't offer a specific indication in that regard —, the general consensus is that they should be considered literary personalities.

12. Fernando Pessoa, *The Selected Prose of Fernando Pessoa*, op. cit., 258–259.

The creation of these non-heteronymic literary personalities covers a wide range of literary creations, ranging from fictional authors with only a few fragments and projects to more complex personalities, with biographies as well as several other kinds of texts. Among these literary personalities one finds a multiplicity of English fictional authors, some of which engage in close dialogue with the works of the writings of the other heteronymic creations. That is the case with I.I. Crosse and Thomas Crosse, who sign texts — included in this edition — that analyze the works of the heteronyms, such as Alberto Caeiro and Álvaro de Campos, and — in the case of Thomas Crosse — even refer to the name of other literary personalities created by Pessoa, such as António Mora, a neo-pagan literary personality entrusted with the task of writing texts about the reconstruction of paganism & creating a philosophical pagan system out of Caeiro's poetry.

Underlying the creation of all of the heteronyms, semi-heteronyms, and literary personalities are the pre-heteronyms. In a letter about the genesis of the heteronyms one reads:

> Ever since I was a child, it has been my tendency to create around me a fictitious world, to surround myself with friends & acquaintances that never existed. (I can't be sure, of course, if they really never existed, or if it's me who doesn't exist. In this matter, as in any

other, we shouldn't be dogmatic.) Ever since I've known myself as "me," I can remember envisioning the shape, motions, character, and life story of various unreal figures who were as visible and as close to me as the manifestations of what we call, perhaps too hastily, real life. This tendency, which goes back as far as I can remember being an I, has always accompanied me, changing somewhat the music it enchants me with, but never the way in which it enchants me.[13]

Recent studies show that Pessoa created more than 100 literary personalities, most of which were produced during the pre-heteronymic period.[14] This creation of pre-heteronyms went through several stages, as Pessoa explicitly asserts in this letter:

This tendency to create around me another world, just like this one but with other people, has never left my imagination. It has gone

13. *Ibid.*, 254–255.

14. See: Fernando Pessoa, *Teoria da Heteronímia*, Fernando Cabral Martins and Richard Zenith (eds) (Lisbon: Assírio & Alvim, 2012); Fernando Pessoa, *Eu sou uma antologia*, *op. cit.* These editions present a revision of Teresa Rita Lopes' seminal work, *Pessoa por Conhecer*, which counts only 72 fictional authors of Pessoa: cf.: Teresa Rita Lopes, *Pessoa por Conhecer*, Vols I & II (Lisbon: Editorial Estampa, 1990).

through various phases, including the one that began in me as a young adult, when a witty remark that was completely out of keeping with who I am or think I am would sometimes and for some unknown reason occur to me, and I would immediately, spontaneously say it as if it came from some friend of mine, whose name I would invent, along with biographical details, and whose figure — physiognomy, stature, dress, & gestures — I would immediately see before me. Thus I elaborated, and propagated, various friends and acquaintances who never existed but whom I feel, hear, and see even today, almost thirty years later. I repeat: I feel, hear, & see them. And I miss them.[15]

It is in the context of the creation of a plural literary space defined by the creation of a plurality of fictional authors that the production of writings on art and poetical theory must be considered. Even in the case of the unsigned texts, we must consider them as multiple perspectives or points of view on different subjects or authors. That change of perspectives is expressed in a text signed by Pessoa in his own name and published,

---

15. Fernando Pessoa, *The Selected Prose of Fernando Pessoa*, op. cit., 255.

in 1915, in a journal, with the title "Crónica da vida que passa" ["Chronicle of the Passing Life"],[16] where one reads:

> A creature of modern nerves, of intelligence without curtains, of awake sensitivity, has the cerebral obligation to change its opinion and certainty several times in the same day. It must have, not religious beliefs, political opinions, literary predilections, but religious sensations, political impressions, impulses of literary admiration.[17]

This text sums up Pessoa's general attitude throughout his work and, therefore, also the attitude present in his theoretical writings on art and poetical theory. Pessoa's poetical theorization is therefore a plural theorization, within a plural literary space.

16. This is the first of a series of chronicles published by Pessoa with the same name in *O Jornal* in 1915. Cf. Fernando Pessoa, *Crítica — Artigos, Ensaios e Entrevista*, ed. Fernando Cabral Martins (Lisbon: Assírio & Alvim, 2000) 105–106; 109–115; 118–121; 527–528; Fernando Pessoa, *Crónicas da Vida que Passa*, ed. Pedro Sepúlveda (Lisbon: Ática, 2011).

17. Fernando Pessoa, *Crítica — Artigos, Ensaios e Entrevista*, op. cit., 105–106.

3 ☞ The Organization of the Texts Collected in this Edition

This edition is divided into two parts. The first part presents a selection of writings on art and poetical theory, originally written by Pessoa in English. It is split into 13 sections: the first five sections contain texts attributed to the various fictional authors created by Pessoa; the following sections corresponding to texts without any signature, but which might be — in their majority — attributed to Pessoa himself. The second part (the "Addenda") contains a set of texts related to those in the first part and which help clarify them.

Part I, section 1 corresponds to a version of the "Essay on Poetry" signed by Professor Trochee. The "Essay on Poetry" is part of a project that Pessoa began to write in his youth, around 1903, while living in Durban, South Africa,[18] and which he brought with him on his return to Portugal, the last fragments being dated approximately around 1906.

The development of the various fragments of the "Essay on Poetry" is complex & multifaceted. The Pessoa

18. Cf. Manuela Parreira da Silva, "Trochee, Prof.," in Fernando Cabral Martins (org.), *Dicionário de Fernando Pessoa e do Modernismo Português* (Lisbon: Editorial Caminho, 2008) 862; Fernando Pessoa, *Teoria da Heteronímia*, op. cit., 61–62; Fernando Pessoa, *Eu Sou Uma Antologia*, op. cit., 170; Fernando Pessoa, *Ensaio sobre Poesia*, ed. Nuno Ribeiro (Lisbon: Apenas Livros, 2020).

Archive contains a multiplicity of testimonies corresponding to different versions, which present several changes ranging from slight modifications of content to the attribution of the authorship of this essay to different pre-heteronyms: first, Doctor Pancratium, whose name appears crossed out in one of the versions of that project; second, Professor Trochee, who subsequently assumes the authorship of the essay; third, Professor Jones, who appears associated with the title of the "Essay on Poetry" in a fragment of the Pessoa Archive; finally, there are two other testimonies without any authorial attribution.

The numerous versions of the fragments of the "Essay on Poetry" can be divided into the following phases:

1) two handwritten testimonies signed by Professor Trochee: first, a fragment (Part I, 1) corresponding to a series of three pages preceded by the name of Professor Trochee written above the name of Doctor Pancratium, which appears crossed out and corresponds to the personality that would initially be responsible for the authorship of the essay but which was later erased by Pessoa; second, a fragment (Part II, 1.1) corresponding to a version of the initial segment of the "Essay on Poetry" signed only by Professor Trochee;

2) a manuscript fragment (Part II, 1.2) with the title "Essay on Poetry" attributed to Professor Jones, but with no other fragment concerning that essay;

3) two testimonies with no authorial attribution: first, a series of 14 handwritten documents (Part II, 1.3);

second, a sequence of three pages (Part II, 1.4) corresponding to a typewritten version of the initial segment
of the text.

Regarding the signature of Professor Trochee in the
version of the "Essay on Poetry" included herein, one reads
the following indication by Manuela Parreira da Silva:

> This fictional personality emerges as the au-
> thor of an *Essay on Poetry — Written for the
> Edification of Would-be Verse Writers*, writ-
> ten in English, probably between 1903 and
> 1905. School calligraphy is clearly the one
> that Pessoa used in Durban. Initially, in the
> known manuscript (PPC 159–162), the text
> is attributed to Doctor Pancratium, a name
> that has been crossed out and replaced by
> that of Prof. Trochee. It is a usual procedure,
> throughout Pessoa's literary life, this fluctu-
> ation or hesitation in the attribution of au-
> thorship of his writings. This may mean that
> Pessoa, after Latinizing his Dr. Pancrácio,
> found it more opportune for the author of an
> essay on rhyme & scansion to have a name
> with a Greek flavor, clearly referring to *tro-
> chee* (foot of Greek-Latin prosody, composed
> of a long syllable and a brief one). The «es-
> say,» included by Pessoa in a list of his works
> as a «humorous» piece, has a humorous tone,

> although it already reveals some of the future
> lines of Pessoa's thought, regarding true poetry.[19]

As Silva clarifies, the "Essay on Poetry" corresponds to a humorous essay on rhyme and scansion, which presents several future lines developed by Pessoa in his poetry, such as the idea that scansion is not at all necessary to a poetical composition, an affirmation that opens the way to the future development of the free verse that would occur in the composition of his heteronyms, namely in Caeiro and Campos.

The second text (Part I, 2) included herein is "Álvaro de Campos is one of the very greatest rhythmists," which is signed by I.I. Crosse. This text corresponds to a presentation of Campos' poetry and was probably meant to divulge abroad the poetical work of this heteronym.

Campos was the first heteronym to appear publicly with the publication of two poems in the modernist literary Portuguese journal *Orpheu*: first, the "Opiary," corresponding to an ode written in rhymed quatrains, as the result of a supposed journey to the Orient; second, the "Triumphal Ode," written in irregular free verse style, which would command most of Campos' poetical compositions, after the influence of Walt Whitman, to whom that heteronym dedicates an ode entitled "Salu-

---

19. Manuela Parreira da Silva, "Trochee, Prof.," in Fernando Cabral Martins (org.), *Dicionário de Fernando Pessoa e do Modernismo Português*, op. cit., 862.

tation to Walt Whitman."[20] Whitman's influence on the poetical compositions of Campos is explicitly stated by Pessoa in this text:

> Álvaro de Campos is excellently defined as a Walt Whitman with a Greek poet inside. He has all the power of intellectual, emotional, and physical sensation that characterised Whitman. But he has the precisely opposite trait — a power of construction and orderly development of a poem that no poet since Milton has attained. Álvaro de Campos' *Triumphal Ode*, which is written in the Whitmanesque absence of stanza and rhyme (and regularity) has a construction and an orderly development which stultifies the perfection that *Lycidas*, for instance, can claim in this particular. The *Naval Ode*, which covers no less than 22 pages of *Orpheu*, is a very marvel of organisation. No German regiment ever had the inner discipline which underlies that composition, which, from its typographical aspect, might almost be considered as a specimen of futurist carelessness.

20. For a better understanding of Whitman's influence throughout Pessoa's work, see: Nuno Ribeiro, Cláudia Souza (eds), *Fernando Pessoa & Walt Whitman* (Lisbon: Apenas Livros, 2018).

The same considerations apply to the magnificent «Salutation to Walt Whitman», in the third *Orpheu*.[21]

In the "Bibliographical Summary" published by Pessoa, one reads as well an important testimony regarding the influence of Whitman on Campos' poetical compositions:

> Álvaro de Campos, born in 1890, isolated the work's (so to speak) emotive side, which he designated as "sensationist" and which — in combination with other, lesser influences, most notably that of Walt Whitman — gave rise to various compositions. These are generally of a scandalous & irritating nature, particularly for Fernando Pessoa, who in any case has no choice but to write and publish them, however much he disagrees with them.[22]

Taking all that has been said into consideration, the text signed by I.I. Crosse describes some of the most important influences in the poetical composition of the heteronym Campos, such as Whitman, and Futurism, the Italian artistic modernist movement.

---

21. Fernando Pessoa, *Páginas Íntimas e de Auto-Interpretação*, Georg Rudolf Lind & Jacinto do Prado Coelho (eds) (Lisbon: Ática, 1966) 142.

22. Fernando Pessoa, *A Little Larger than the Entire Universe*, op. cit., 3.

The third text (Part I, 3) herein, "Cæiro and the Pagan Reaction," is also signed by I.I. Crosse. This essay corresponds to the beginning of an unfinished text that was supposed to present the work of Cæiro in the context of Pessoa's project of creating a Portuguese neo-paganism. The neo-paganism created by Pessoa would revolve around the heteronym Cæiro, who was conceived by the Portuguese author as the master of the heteronyms, and even of the orthonym, as one reads in the letter about the genesis of the heteronyms, where Pessoa describes the mythical triumphal day — "March 8th, 1914" — that narrates the creation of the heteronyms:

> (...) it was March 8th, 1914 — I walked over to a high chest of drawers, took a sheet of paper, and began to write standing up, as I do whenever I can. And I wrote thirty-some poems at once, in a kind of ecstasy I'm unable to describe. It was the triumphal day of my life, and I can never have another one like it. I began with a title, *The Keeper of Sheep*. This was followed by the appearance in me of someone whom I instantly named Alberto Caeiro. Excuse the absurdity of this statement: my master had appeared in me. (...)

> Once Alberto Cæiro had appeared, I instinctively and subconsciously tried to find disciples for him. From Cæiro's false paganism I

extracted the latent Ricardo Reis, at last discovering his name and adjusting him to his
true self, for now I actually saw him. And
then a new individual, quite the opposite
of Ricardo Reis, suddenly and impetuously
came to me. In an unbroken stream, without
interruptions or corrections, the ode whose
name is "Triumphal Ode," by the man whose
name is none other than Álvaro de Campos,
issued from my typewriter.[23]

This passage briefly outlines the relation between the
heteronyms and Caeiro's paganism. A more explicit
account of this is asserted in *Notes for the Memory of
My Master Caeiro*, signed by the heteronym Campos,
who says:

My master Cæiro wasn't a pagan; he was
paganism. Ricardo Reis is a pagan, António
Mora is a pagan, and I'm a pagan; Fernando
Pessoa himself would be a pagan, were he not
a ball of string inwardly wound around itself.
But Ricardo Reis is a pagan by virtue of his
character, António Mora is a pagan by virtue
of his intellect, and I'm a pagan out of sheer
revolt, i.e. by my temperament. For Cæiro's

23. Fernando Pessoa, *The Selected Prose of Fernando Pessoa*, op.
cit., 256.

paganism there was no explanation; there
was consubstantiation.[24]

Thus, "Cæiro and the Pagan Reaction," which is signed
by I.I. Crosse, must be considered in the context of Pessoa's defense and creation of a Portuguese neo-pagan
movement.

The fourth text (Part I, 4) of part one corresponds to
the only fragment explicitly signed by Thomas Crosse
to a preface for the English translation of Cæiro's poetry.
Thomas Crosse is an overly complex and multifarious
literary personality. He was not only conceived as the
translator and presenter into English of Cæiro's poetry,
but also as the author of several texts and articles.[25] In
a list from the Pessoa Archive one finds the following
reference to Thomas Crosse as translator of Cæiro's poetry: «"Complete Poems of Alberto Cæiro." Tradução
Thomas Crosse.»[26] The text presented in part I, section

24. *Ibid.*, 40.

25. For further information on this, see: Teresa Rita Lopes, *Pessoa
    por Conhecer*, op. cit., 118–128; Teresa Rita Lopes, *Pessoa por
    Conhecer*, vol. II, op. cit., 233–234; Fernando Pessoa, *Teoria da
    Heteronímia*, op. cit., 95–96; Fernando Pessoa, *Eu sou uma antologia*, op. cit., 475–490; Pedro Sepúlveda, Jorge Uribe, "Planeamento editorial de uma obra em potência: o autor, crítico e
    tradutor Thomas Crosse," in: *Revista Colóquio / Letras*, № 183
    (2013) 57–79; Fernando Pessoa, *A Família Crosse*, Nuno Ribeiro
    and Cláudia Souza (eds) (Lisbon: Apenas Livros, 2019).

26. Fernando Pessoa, *A Família Crosse*, op. cit., 48.

4, corresponds to the fragment for the preface to that translation.

The fragment of the preface to Cæiro's poetry signed by Thomas Crosse must be considered in the context of Pessoa's neo-paganism. One important aspect in that text corresponds to the reference to António Mora, which dialogues with the works of the heteronyms. This literary personality was meant to be the author of several books about the reconstruction of paganism and was a disciple of Cæiro.[27] Though Pessoa never publishes any of his projected works, there is a reference to this personality in an excerpt (quoted above) of the *Notes for the Memory of My Master Cæiro* published, in 1931, under the name of Álvaro de Campos in number 30 of *Presença*.

Section five (Part I, 5) contains two fragments — under the title "The Similarity of Spanish and Portuguese" — that present Pessoa's considerations on the comparison of different languages, signed by Thomas Crosse. One of the most relevant dimensions of Pessoa's writings on art and poetical theory corresponds to his texts about the Portuguese language and its similarities or differences regarding the specificity of

27. These fragments are housed in the Pessoa Archive. For two important editions containing Mora's texts, see: Fernando Pessoa, *Obras de António Mora*, ed. Luís Filipe B. Teixeira (Lisbon: Imprensa Nacional-Casa da Mœda, 2002); Fernando Pessoa, *O Regresso dos Deuses e Outros Escritos de António Mora* (Lisbon: Assírio & Alvim, 2013).

other languages.[28] Though Pessoa doesn't leave any specific title in his original documents, one finds in Thomas Crosse's lists of possible articles two titles that might correspond to ones intended to be attributed to these texts: 1) "The conflict of languages and the universal language";[29] 2) "Singularities of language."[30]

The texts signed by Thomas Crosse begin with an analysis of the similarities between the Spanish and Portuguese languages, & the sequence of the thesis developed in that literary personality's documents about the languages, extent to the analysis of other languages such as English, French, Italian, and even a comparison between Brazilian Portuguese and the Portuguese spoken in Portugal, as well as an analysis of Spanish as spoken throughout several Spanish-speaking countries.

Section six (Part I, 6) contains a series of fragments entitled "Impermanence" that deal with the survival of literary works. Throughout the Pessoa Archive one finds several writings and projects concerning this.[31] The group of fragments preceded by the title "Impermanence" is one of Pessoa's more significant projects

---

28. A relevant edition about Portuguese in comparison to other languages is: Fernando Pessoa, *A Língua Portuguesa*, ed. Luísa Medeiros (Lisbon: Assírio & Alvim, 1997).

29. Fernando Pessoa, *A Família Crosse*, op. cit., 43.

30. *Ibid.*, 44.

31. See: Fernando Pessoa, *Heróstrato e a Busca da Imortalidade*, ed. Richard Zenith (Lisbon: Assírio & Alvim, 2000).

in this regard. At the beginning of the first fragment presented herein, Pessoa establishes the premises:

> The problem of the survival of literary works, and of the permanent elements of literature is, after all, a very simple one. All life is adaptation to environment, and all death inadaptation to it.
>
> A work of art is therefore living or great by its approval as great by a critical environment.[32]

The sequence of the other fragments develops the degrees and conditions of adaptation or inadaptation and approval or disapproval of a literary work, establishing a detailed account of the criteria necessary to the survival or death of a work and defending the idea that the wider the cultural environment a certain literary work adapts to, the more chances it will have to survive.

Section seven (Part I, 7) presents a brief text titled "Uselessness of Criticism." This text deals specifically with the problem concerning the criteria of critical literary activity. Throughout his life, Pessoa wrote several texts on literary criticism, some of which he published,[33] about other authors, so his interest in examining the

---

32. BNP/E3, 19 — 79ʳ.

33. The collection of theoretical texts on literary criticism published during his life can be found in: Fernando Pessoa, *Crítica — Ensaios, Artigos e Entrevistas*, op. cit.

conditions of the critical activity of literature is concordant with his general activities. The "Uselessness of Criticism" addresses precisely these questions: "For how is a critic to judge? What are the qualities that make, not the casual, but the competent critic?"[34] Taking these concerns into consideration, that text highlights the difficulty of judging the quality & originality of contemporary works, as we see here:

> On every side we hear the cry that the age needs a great poet. The central hollowness of all modern achievement is a thing rather felt than spoken about..... If the great poet were to appear, who would be where to notice him? Who can say whether he has not already appeared? The reading public sees in the papers notices of the work of those men whose influence and friendships have made them known, or whose secondariness has made them accepted of the crowd. The great poet may have appeared already; his work will have been noticed in a few "vient-de-paraître" words in some bibliographic summary of a critical paper.[35]

Section eight (Part I, 8) corresponds to the transcription of the two fragments from the text "Three Pessimists."

34. BNP/E3, 18 — 42ʳ.
35. *Ibid.*

The three pessimists Pessoa refers to are: 1) the Italian writer Giacomo Leopardi; 2) the French Romantic poet Alfred de Vigny; and 3) Antero de Quental, one of the most important XIXth century Portuguese writers, mostly known as a poet, but whose work presents, as well, relevant philosophical works in the context of Portuguese culture. In the "Three Pessimists," Pessoa analyzes Leopardi, Vigny, and Antero as "victims of the Romantic illusion":[36]

> The Romantic illusion consists in taking literally the Greek philosopher's phrase that man is the measure of all things, or sentimentally the basic affirmation of the critical philosophy, that all the world is a concept of ours. These affirmations, harmless to the mind in themselves, are particularly dangerous, and often absurd, when they become dispositions of temperament and not merely concepts of the mind.[37]

The three pessimists are here referred to as victims because, although none of them had a Romantic temperament — "All three were destined to be classicists,"[38] says Pessoa — they were still prey to the Romantic illusion.

36. BNP/E3, 14D — 23[r].

37. *Ibid.*

38. *Ibid.*

This tension between classicism and a Romantic temperament is the motto of the fragments destined to the "Three Pessimists."

Section nine (Part I, 9) presents several sequences of documents[39] from the Pessoa Archive about the poem "Antinous," an English poem published by Pessoa during his life. These sequences of documents deal with the problem of morality and immorality in art, taking the subject of the poem as a starting point. The poem "Antinous" deals with the homoerotic love relationship between the Roman Emperor Adrian and his deceased boyfriend "Antinous." Pessoa argues that the morality or immorality, not only of his poem but also of poetry in general, is not an argument against the aesthetic value of an artistic creation. In "Pessoa's Antinous," J.D. Reed provides the following account of this poem's relevance in the context of the English literary tradition:

> For the student of Classical reception, Pessoa's *Antinous* (1918), with its picture of the Roman emperor Hadrian's grief for his dead boyfriend, caps a roster of nineteenth-century English poems inspired by "dying god" figures, Greek mythological characters like Adonis, beloved by a powerful deity, lost objects of beauty. Examples are Shelley's "Adonais," his elegy on Keats under the guise

39. BNP/E3, 14A — 7–10, 14A — 1–3, 14A — 4–6.

of an Adonis-figure; Keats's own "Endymion," particularly the Adonis section; Swinburne's take on the Tannhäuser legend, "Laus Veneris," with its heated eroticism & hopeless roster of the vampiric Venus' cast-off lovers. The "Epitaph on Adonis" of the ancient Greek poet Bion of Smyrna (late second century BCE) lies in the background, as it does for those poems, too; more generally felt is the tradition of the "pastoral lament" from Theocritus' "Idyll 1" through the anonymous "Epitaph for Bion" (a principal influence on Shelley) to Milton's "Lycidas." The echœs I hear — both surface echœs and those in the underlying poetics — are perhaps products of my own filters (which, to be sure, screen out as much as they screen in), but I hope to show that that literary background is an apt one.[40]

Two different versions of the Poem "Antinous" were published during Pessoa's life: first, an author edition, published in 1918;[41] second, as the first part of the *English Poems I–II*,[42] published in 1921 by *Olisipo*, a publishing house created by Pessoa, which was active between 1921 and 1923. In the addenda to this edition, we include the

40. J.D. Reed, "Pessoa's Antinous," in *Pessoa Plural*: 10 (O./Fall 2016) 107.

41. Fernando Pessoa, *Antinous* (Lisbon: Monteiro & Co., 1918).

42. Fernando Pessoa, *English Poems I–II* (Lisbon: Olisipo, 1921).

second version of that poem so that the reader may understand the sequence of texts about "Antinous" in relation to that poem. In the second version of "Antinous" (1921), Pessoa includes the following note:

> An early & very imperfect draft of *Antinous* was published in 1918. The present one is meant to annul and supersede that, from which is essentially different.[43]

Taking this note into consideration, we've decided to present the transcription of the second version of that poem, published in 1921, for Pessoa explicitly says that this version was supposed to *annul and supersede* the first one published in 1918.

Section ten (Part I, 10) presents a selection of Pessoa's English writings on sensationism, a Portuguese literary movement he created.[44] This section contains two subsections: the first is a letter to an English publisher proposing the publication of an Anthology of Portuguese "sensationist" poetry, where Pessoa sums up the

43. *Ibid.*, 4.

44. One finds an extensive collection of Pessoa's sensationist writings in: Fernando Pessoa, *Sensacionismo e Outros Ismos*, ed. Jerónimo Pizarro (Lisbon: Imprensa Nacional — Casa da Moeda, 2009). For an important study about the relation between Pessoa and the sensationist movement see: José Gil, *Fernando Pessoa ou la Métaphysique des Sensations* (Paris: Éditions de la Différence, 1988).

main principles of sensationism; the second is a collection of fragments, written originally in English, about the sensationist movement, which probably correspond to outlines for future divulgation abroad.

Sensationism is a literary and philosophical movement conceived by Pessoa, based on a distinctive philosophical position created by him that takes sensation as the essential reality for us and the point of departure for artistic creation, as he explicitly asserts when characterizing the "central attitude of sensationism": "The only reality in life is sensation. The only reality in art is consciousness of the sensation."[45] Taking this principle as a starting point, Pessoa creates sensationism on the one hand, to give a certain unity to the multiplicity of literary movements that were emerging in Portugal in his time and, on the other hand, to justify the development of a plurality of styles in his own work. Indeed, the sensationist movement is conceived by Pessoa in the following fragment as a cosmopolitan artistic movement, that is, as a movement that admits all styles and doesn't assume an attitude of exclusion regarding the criteria of the establishment of aesthetic feeling:

> Sensationism differs from common literary currents in that it is not exclusive, that is to say, it does not claim for itself the monopoly of right aesthetic feeling. Properly speaking,

45. BNP/E3, 20 — 87ʳ.

it does not claim for itself that it is, except in a certain restricted sense, a current or a movement, but only partly an attitude, and partly an addition to all preceding currents.[46]

The relation between sensationism and the literary tradition is therefore an inclusive relation of synthesis regarding the features of earlier literary movements:

The sensationist movement (represented by the Lisbon quarterly "Orpheu") represents the final synthesis. It gathers into one organic whole (for a synthesis is not a sum) the several threads of modern movements, extracting honey from all the flowers that have blossomed in the gardens of European fancy.[47]

But the relation between sensationism and the literary tradition is not one of pure and simple acceptance and inclusion of all aspects of earlier literary movements. Sensationism only accepts the affirmative aspects of the preceding literary movements, that is, all the aspects that don't limit artistic creation, excluding their negative and exclusionary sides, as one reads in the following passage that compares the sensationist aesthetic attitude to the philosophy of Spinoza:

46. BNP/E3, 20 — 114^r.

47. BNP/E3, 88 — 31^r.

> Spinoza said that philosophical systems are
> right in what they affirm and wrong in what
> they deny. This, the greatest of all pantheistic
> affirmations, is what sensationism can repeat
> in relation to æsthetic things.[48]

Thus, the cosmopolitan and inclusive aspects of sensationism, that is, the fact that it accepts the affirmative side of all earlier literary movements and doesn't claim for itself neither the monopoly of a right way of feeling nor of a right way of writing, are the principles for the constitution of Pessoa's sensationist movement.

Section eleven (Part I, 11) presents a group of texts focusing on the definition and characterizing features of art and poetry. In the Pessoa Archive one finds several documents about this subject that correspond to observations about the scope of artistic & poetical activities and which were probably conceived as something that Pessoa intended to further develop in longer texts. These texts document Pessoa's considerations about the definition of art and its relations to and differences from philosophy, morality, religion, & science, as well as the role of art in society and the attempt to define what poetry is.

Section twelve (Part I, 12) presents a fragment on translation. As noted, the relation between Pessoa & translation is multifarious. He not only worked in

48. BNP/E3, 20 — 114[r].

Lisbon as a translator of commercial letters, but he also published translations into Portuguese. Considering such, Pessoa's interest in theorizing translation is not out of character but in line with his expansive approach to writing. This text deals with the problem concerning the "mental processes involved in translating well"[49] and can be considered as a poetic art of translation in the context of Pessoa's work.

Section thirteen (Part I, 13) contains a selection of fragments on a number of British writers ranging from the 16th to the 20th century. One finds in Pessoa's writings several clues that enable one to understand the impact of English literature on his work. He not only read several works of English literature, but also wrote about that literary tradition. Among the documents present in the Pessoa Archive it is possible to identify, for example, several testimonies regarding the project of an actual "História da Literatura Inglesa" ["History of English Literature"] that Pessoa planned to write in Portuguese, but never came to finish. Besides this project, one finds, as well, several pages written originally in English with critical comments on several English writers. In section 13 herein, we present some of the most significant pages with texts about nine authors: Shakespeare, Milton, Burns, Shelley, Keats, Tennyson, Dickens, Wilde, and Francis Thompson.

---

49. BNP/E3, 14[1] — 99[r].

4 ☞ Criteria of Publication and Provenance of the Texts

This edition presents a transcription of a selection of Pessoa's writings on art and poetical theory, which were originally written in English and are held at the Fernando Pessoa Archive in Biblioteca Nacional de Portugal (BNP). In transcribing this material, we have always kept the first version of a word or sentence wherever there is more than one variant. We've adopted this criterion since, in many cases, Pessoa left more than one variant for a word or sentence without indicating his preference, for he never made a final and complete version of these texts, with the exception of the poem "Antinous" (Part II, 2). All of the struck-out segments are excluded from the text, since Pessoa intentionally expressed that wish, but misspellings have been corrected. Wherever we introduce a correction in the text for grammatical reasons, we indicate the original sentence or segment in a footnote. For the transcription of these texts, we use the following symbols:

XXXXXX underlined segment
☐ empty space left by the author

Acknowledgments

We are grateful to FCT — Foundation for the Science & Technology —, which currently finances — under the program of FSE — the post-doctoral research project of Nuno Ribeiro (SFRH/BPD/121514/2016) on the Pessoa Archive, in IELT — Institute for the Study of Literature and Tradition, Faculty of Social and Human Sciences — New University of Lisbon, & to CFUL — Centre of Philosophy of the University of Lisbon —, where Cláudia Souza develops her current research. We are also grateful to Professor Fernando Cabral Martins for institutional support.

I

Writings on Art and Poetical Theory

1 ☞ Professor Trochee: Essay on Poetry

[100 — 4–6]

Essay on Poetry
Written for the edification of would-be verse-writers
by Professor Trochee [50]

When I consider the superabundance of young men *&*
the great number of young women in the present century, when I survey the necessary and consequent profusion of reciprocal attachments, when I reflect upon the
exuberance of poetical compositions emanating therefrom, when I bring my mind to bear upon the insanity and chaotic formation of these effusions, I convince
myself that, by writing a good and convenient essay on
the poetical art, I shall be greatly contributing to the
emolument of the public.

Having, therefore, carefully considered the best and
most practical way in which to open such a relevant discussion, I have most wisely concluded that a straightforward exposition of the rules and exceptions of poetry is the manner in which I shall present my most

---

50. In the original document, one reads: "*By Professor Trochee / By
~~Doctor Pancratium~~*." This indicates that this fragment version of
the *Essay on Poetry* was first attributed to the pre-heteronym
Doctor Pancratium and only, afterwards, to Professor Trochee.

orthodox ideas to the patient readers. I have thought it useless and inappropriate to refer myself too often to the ancient critics on the art discussed, one of my reasons for so doing being that I am unacquainted with anything beyond their names. I must therefore ask my kindly readers to appeal, during the perusal of this composition, to their common sense, or to whatever mental faculty occupies in their brains the place taken in ordinary mortals by that quality.

Firstly, I think it proper to bring to the notice of the would-be poet a fact which is not usually considered and yet is deserving of consideration. I hope I shall escape universal ridicule if I assert that poetry should, be susceptible of scansion. I wish it, of course, to be understood that I agree with □ in maintaining that strict scansion is not at all necessary for the success nor even for the merit of a poetical composition. And I trust I shall not be deemed exceedingly pedantic if I delve into the storehouse of time to produce, as an authority, some of the works of a certain William Shakespeare, or Shakspeare, who lived some centuries ago and even enjoyed some reputation as a dramatist. This person used often to take off, or add on, one syllable or more in the lines of his numerous productions, and, if it be at all allowable in the age of Kipling to break the tenets of poetical good-sense by imitating some obscure scribbler, I should dare to recommend to the beginner the enjoyment of this sort of poetic licence. Not that I should advise him to *add* any syllables to his lines, but the subtraction of some is often convenient and desirable. I may as well point out that if, by this very contrivance, the young poet, having taken away some syllables from his poem, proceed on this expedient, and take all the remaining syllables out of it, although he might not thus attain to any degree of popularity, he nevertheless would exhibit an extraordinary amount of poetical common sense. If the poem under question be dedicated to some nymph or naiad, this magnificent condensation may not please her, but do you merely remind her that, if she will not accept the remainder of the poem, that is to say, your name, her love for you is not the thing you expected.

There are not many other useful remarks that I can make upon scansion; I might, of course, spend nights and days in the process of demonstrating to you its various eccentricities, but, since that would only be wasting your patience and my time, I beg, therefore, to proceed □

Facsimiles of the *Essay on Poetry* Version
signed by Professor Trochee

[BNP / E3, 100 — 4ʳ: facsimile]

1.   100-4

Essay on Poetry   poetie

Written for the Edification of Would-be Verse writers
By Professor Trochee
~~By Doctor Provocatium~~

When I consider the superabundance of young men and the great number of young women in the present century, when I survey the necessary and consequent profusion of reciprocal attachments, when I reflect upon the exuberance of poetical compositions emanating therefrom, when I bring my mind to bear upon the insanity and chaotic formation of these effusions, I convince myself that, by writing a good and convenient essay on the poetical art, I shall be really contributing to the emolument of the public.

Having, therefore, carefully considered the best and most practical way in which to open such a relevant discussion, I have most wisely concluded that a straightforward exposition of the rules and exceptions of poetry is the manner in which I shall present my most orthodox ideas ~~offering~~ to the patient readers. I have thought it useless and inappropriate to refer myself too often to the ancient critics on the art discussed, one of my reasons for so doing being that I am unacquainted with anything beyond their names. I must therefore ask my kindly readers to appeal, during the perusal of this composition, to their common sense, or to whatever mental faculty occupies in their brains the place taken in ordinary mortals' by that quality.

Firstly, I think it proper to bring to the notice of the would-be poet a fact which is not usually considered and yet ~~deserves~~ ↑deserving↓ ~~from~~ ~~much~~ consideration. I hope I shall escape universal ridicule if I assert that poetry should, ~~generally~~ ↑not really↓ scan. I wish it, of course, to be understood that I agree with ~~Mr. Edward~~ ~~Lewis~~ in maintaining that strict scansion is not at all necessary for the success ↑or even for the merit↓ of a poetical composition ↑and↓. I trust I shall not be deemed exceedingly pedantic if I delve into the storehouse of time to produce, as an authority, some of the works of a certain William Shakspeare, ↑Shakespeare,↓ ~~Shakspere↓~~ Shakespear &c, who lived some centuries ago and even enjoyed some reputation as a dramatist. This person used often to take off or add on, one syllable or more in the lines of his numerous productions, and, if it be at all allowable in the age of Kipling to break the tenets of poetical good-sense by imitating some obscure scribbler, I should dare to re-commend to the beginner the enjoyment of this sort of poetical licence. Not that I should advise him to add any syllables to his lines, but the subtraction of some is often convenient and desirable. I may as well point out that if, by this very contrivance, the young poet, having taken away some syllables from his poem, proceed on this expedient, and take all the remaining syllables out of it, although he might not thus attain to any degree of popularity, he nevertheless would exhibit an extraordinary amount of poetical common sense. If the ~~poem~~ under question be dedicated to some nymph or naiad, this magnificent condensation may not please her, but do you merely remind her that, if she will not accept the re-

mainder of the poem, that is to say, your name, her love for you
is not the thing you expected.

There are not many other useful remarks that I can make
upon scansion; I might, of course, spend nights and days in the
process of demonstrating to you its various eccentricities, but, since
that would only be wasting your patience and my time, I beg, therefore, to proceed.

2 ☞ I. I. Crosse: "Álvaro de Campos is one of the very greatest rhythmists"

[14A — 66–67]

I. I. Crosse

Álvaro de Campos is one of the very greatest rhythmists that there has ever been. Every metric paragraph of his is a finished work of art. He makes definite, perfectly "curved" stanzas of these irregular "meters."

He is the most violent of all writers. His master Whitman is mild and calm compared to him. Yet the more turbulent of the 2 poets is the most self-controlled. He is so violent that enough of the energy of his violence remains to him to use it in disciplining his violence.

The violence of the *Naval Ode* is perfectly insane. Yet it is unparalleled in art, and because its violence is such.

His volcanic emotion, his violence of sensation, his formidable shifting from violence to tenderness, from a passion for great and loud things to a love of humble and quiet ones, his unparalleled transitions, his sudden silences, sudden pauses… his change from unstable to equable states of mind — none has ever approached him in the □ of this hysteria of our age.

8

The classic training of his early years, that never deserts him (for he is one of the most unified of poets, and ever a builder and a fitter-together of parts in an organic whole); his individual stability, his mathematical training and scientific training, adding another stabilizing influence (never too much for such a volcanic temperament) □

His feverous contempt of small things, of small people, of all our age, because it is composed of small things and of small people.

This quasi-Futurist who loves the great classical poets because they were great and despises the literary men of his time because they are all small.

His art of conveying sensations by a single stroke:

A fita cor de rosa deixada em cima da cómoda,

O último brinquedo partido (comboio ainda
    com a fita suja para o puxar)

Da criança inevitavelmente morta, ó mãe de
    preto a dobrar-lhe o fato.

[The pink ribbon left on top of the dresser,
The last broken toy (train still with dirty tape
    to pull it)
Of the child inevitably dead, o mother dressed
    in black folding the suit.]

His terrible self-analysis, making suddenly cold all his emotion, as in the "Salutation."

Facsimile of the First Page of
"Álvaro de Campos is one of the very greatest rhythmists"

[BNP / E3, 14A — 66ʳ: facsimile]

3 ☞ I. I. Crosse: Cæiro and the Pagan Reaction

[143 — 7–9]

I. I. Crosse.

Cæiro and the Pagan Reaction

The first qualification for a critic of science or of art, that is to say, of an intellectual production which strives for an absolute value (truth or beauty) is that he should be able to distinguish between relative and absolute values. When a work of art pleases him, when he feels it is beautiful, his first intellectual movement, after that movement of sensibility, should be to ask himself: Do I find this beautiful as a man, or as a man of my time, or as a man of my country? Does this appeal, really, to the man in me, or to the modern man in me, or the Englishman, or Frenchman, or Italian that I am?

Very few are able to undertake such self-analysis, but we are optimistic enough about mankind to believe that the greater number of clever men are not able to undertake it because they have never been taught that they ought to undertake it.

If this principle of self-criticism before criticism of others, of analysis of impressions before analysis of the results of impressions, were more commonly put into practice, we would have been spared many follies. As it

is the sage of looking back at 40 on the foolish enthusiasm of 20 has no equal since the looking back at 60
to the equally foolish, though seeming-cooler, enthusiasm of 40.

I have even held it necessary to take this mental
attitude. So when I first read Alberto Cæiro, I felt the
enthusiasm of □

Here at last — said I to myself — is a work that ap-
peals to me not as a man of to-day (no work could be
further removed from every known current of contemporary art), not as an Englishman (no work could be
less English), but indeed as a man of mankind.

The more I analysed my feelings, the more I came to
accept this conclusion of mine as true.

I am not so bold of my real opinion of Cæiro's works,
as to tell the reader frankly how much I think of him.

> The great discovery of Cæiro — the mysti-
> cism of objectivity. As mystics see meaning
> in all things, Cæiro, in his own words, sees
> lack of meaning in all things,

See it and I love myself, because to be a thing is to
mean nothing.

Facsimile of the First Page of
Cæiro and the Pagan Reaction

[BNP / E3, 143 — 7ʳ: facsimile]

I. I. Crosse.

Cæiro & the Pagan
Reaction

The first qualification for a
critic of science or of art, that
is to say, of an intellectual
production which strives for an
absolute value (truth or
beauty) is that he should be
able to distinguish between relation & absolute values, ~~but
he should have it in view to
distinguish~~ when a work of
art pleases him, when he
feels it is beautiful, his first
intellectual movement, after
that movement of the sensibility, should be to ask himself: Do I find this beautiful
as a man, or as a man of
my time, or as a man of
my country? Does this appeal,

4 ☞ Thomas Crosse: Alberto Cæiro — Translator's Preface

[143 — 1–4]

Th. Crosse

But Cæiro displaces all our mental habits and puts all our notions out of drowsing.

He does it, first of all, by the philosophy which can hardly be said to be simply "at the bottom" of his poetry, because it is both at the bottom and at the top of it. Whatever a mystic may be, he is certainly a kind of mystic. But he is, not only a materialistic mystic, which is already strange enough, but still can be imagined, for there is some sort of a modern precedent in Nietzsche and of an ancient one in some Greeks, but a non-subjectivistic mystic, which is quite bewildering. Some of those ancient Greeks, already referred to, are something like that, but it is so difficult to conceive a recent "modern" being precisely like a primitive Greek, that we are not at all aided by the very analogy that does at first seem to help us.

Cæiro puts us out, next, by the secondary aspects of his philosophy. Being a poet of what may be called "the absolute Concrete" he never looks on that concrete *otherwise than abstractly*. No man is more sure of the absolute, unsubjective reality of a tree, of a stone, of a flower. How it might be thought that he would particularize, that he would say "an oak," "a round stone," "a marigold." But he does not: he keeps on saying "a tree," "a stone," "a flower."

All these observations will be better understood after reading the poems.

But, if the matter is thus perplexing, the manner is more perplexing still.

The intellectual manner, to begin with. There is nothing less poetic, less lyrical than Cæiro's philosophical attitude. It is quite devoid of "imagination," of vagueness, of "sympathy" with things. Far from "feeling" them, his mental process, a hundred times explicitly put, is that he does not feel them, or feel with them.

Again, his simplicity is full of intellectual complexity. He is a poet purely of sense, but he seems to have his intellect put into his senses.

Then, again, his is absolutely self-conscious. He knows every possible weakness of his. Where there may be a logical fault, he hastens to the rescue with a simple & direct argument. Where □

This man, so purely an ancient — nay, a primitive — Greek that he is bewildering, is quite "modern" at the same time.

It is this man of contradictions, this lucidly muddled personality that gives him his complex & intense originality — an originality, in every way, scarcely ever attained by any poet; certainly never before attained by a poet born in a worn and sophisticated age.

Dr. Antonio Mora,[51] explaining him on the lines of a similar philosophy — on discipular lines, perhaps — has left this aspect of him out; and that is why I do not feel it supererogatory to call attention to it. Dr. Mora is also a Pagan, in the same complete and Greek sense that Cæiro is a Pagan. So, to Dr. Mora, Cæiro is a great poet, but hardly a *strange* poet. He is great because he has brought back the Pagan sense of the world; he is not strange because Dr. Mora thinks the Pagan sense of the world a *possible* sense in our time. Now the great point is that the Pagan sense of the world is impossible; and the formidable (there is no other word) originality of Cæiro lies in that he has realized this impossibility.

51. António Mora is a literary personality created by Fernando Pessoa. He was meant to be — along with Ricardo Reis, Álvaro de Campos, and Fernando Pessoa — a disciple of the heteronym Alberto Cæiro. Pessoa entrusts Mora with the task of reducing into a philosophical system the thought present in the poetry of the master Cæiro. In the Pessoa Archive one finds several fragments about the reconstruction of paganism, which correspond to the attempt of philosophically explaining Cæiro's poems. Although Pessoa did not publish during his life the writings of Mora, one finds a reference to him in the text *Notas para a Recordação do Meu Mestre Cæiro* [*Notes for the Memory of My Master Cæiro*] signed by the heteronym Campos and published before Pessoa's death.

No theory of reincarnation can take him in. He is not the soul of a primitive Greek brought into a modern to-day; he is altogether a great Greek, more truly Greek than most Greek poets, & what there is modern in him is only the inscrutable part, as inscrutable as lies nothing in Portugal, being born from a Portuguese.

He has the Greek sense of proportion without the Greek sense of form. His poems are written in irregular, unrhythmic lines; they are of any length, like Whitman's, and they are less rhythmic in their paragraphs, being, each of them, fault bad ear. But the poems are faultless as to proportion, not one line is too much, not one word is misplaced, not one interpretation is made.

The clear □ thought, the □ emotion of this poet whose characteristic affirmations are represented by that verse that a stone is more real than an emotion, & that biting a fruit is the only way of *thinking it*.

5 ☞ Thomas Crosse: "The Similarity of Spanish and Portuguese"

[143 — 13–14]⁵²

The similarity of Spanish and Portuguese is perhaps not easily imagined by anyone unacquainted with either or both; and I say "either or both" because to be acquainted with one is practically to be acquainted with the other. But a common phrase will show the close resemblance. Take the phrase "I have received your letter and thank you for it." Put down, one under the other the Spanish and the Portuguese for that; here they are:

Spanish: Recebí su carta, que agradezco.

Portuguese: Recebi sua carta, que agradeço.

52. *In the beginning of this document — before the text about* "The Similarity of Spanish and Portuguese" — *one reads the following list of possible articles, which Pessoa intended to write under the name of Thomas Crosse:*

Thomas Crosse's possible articles:

1. The conflict of languages and the universal language.
2. The birthplace of Columbus.
3. Epigrams.
4. Dictatorships.
5. King Sebastian.
6. The Legend of the Returning King.
7. The Old Portuguese Song-Books.
8. The Military Government in Portugal (based on Interregno).

[BNP/E3, 143 — 13]

Barring a letter or two, the words are the same. This is not so throughout the two languages, of course; there are surprising differences, chiefly in common words. But the fact remains that if you read one language, you can automatically understand anything written in the other; and if you speak one, you will be understood by anyone speaking the other, if you do not speak too quickly. The Portuguese automatically read and understand Spanish better and quicker than the Spanish-speaking peoples understand Portuguese; that is because Portuguese is the more difficult and complex, besides being by far the richer, of the two, and because the Portuguese are far more pliant and adaptable than the Spanish.

The final conflict between English and Spanish and Portuguese will resolve itself into

(1) England has a far greater and more varied literature than both Spain and Portugal put together.

(2) Portuguese was brought in the seventeenth century to a degree of exactness, purity and perfection which Spanish never attained and English seems never to have neared attaining.

(3) To-day, in spite of common English, common Spanish, and common Portuguese being equally flagrant departures from pure speech, yet the Portuguese react more against this, and the best Portuguese writers of to-day, however little they may be important intellectually, do write their language better than the best English and the best Spanish writers write theirs.

(4) English is more complex and concise than either Spanish or Portuguese. On the other hand, Portuguese has possibilities of shades of meaning which are undreamed of even in English. The Portuguese have, for instance, a personal infinitive. Thus the phrase which in English cannot be rendered in less words than "It is enough that we exist" or "that we be," can be given in Portuguese in only two words — "Basta sermos."

French has the advantage of its great simplicity. It has a very easy grammar, its rules are very simple and it is not difficult with some care to write it with at least comparative purity.

[143 — 10–12]

Th. Cr.

The fatal drawback of Spanish psychology (?) seems to be their tendency to division. This is very clearly seen in South America. Whereas the Portuguese part, enormous as it is in territory, has kept one under the name of Brazil, the Spanish portion has split up into several republics. This cannot be said to be a reflex of the essential division of Spain itself, for the two divisions are of a different type. The division of Spain proceeds from the fact that it incorporates several nations, speaking different languages, and not merely different dialects — Catalonia, the Basque Provinces and Galicia, neither of which have Spanish as a natural language; the rest may be considered as "conquered." But the division of Spanish America does not derive from any linguistic origin, for throughout those territories, it is Spanish, i.e. Castilian, which is spoken. Separatism seems to be, for some unknown reason, a Spanish characteri[stic].

For our present case, all depends on how far this division will influence any possible linguistic division. There is a tendency to linguistic division in all the American continent. We all know and see how the English spoken in America is departing from British English. But the same thing happens in respect of Spanish and Portuguese in the other parts of the Continent. The divergence between the Spanish of Spanish America and the Spanish of Spain is varying; it is greater in some regions than in others, as might be supposed. The divergence between Brazilian and European Portuguese is similarly divergent in respect of the various provinces which make up Brazil. But whereas in North America there is very little reaction in favour of "pure English undefiled," and in Spanish America very little in the same sense with regard to Spanish, in Brazil there is and has always been a strong "classical" current. As a matter of fact, the best Brazilian Writers (except in such cases as the great poet Catulo Cearense,[53] who

---

53. Catulo da Paixão Cearense (1863–1946) was a Brazilian writer and musician, known as one of the most significant popular song composers.

dramatizes his poems in the patois of the Brazilian Backwoods) are particularly scrupulous in the use of Portuguese and write more classically and more near to the Vieira standard than the best writers in Portugal. Again, Brazilian newspapers are generally written in better Portuguese than the Portuguese papers, which are in the main deplorably anti-national in this respect. That is to say, the Portuguese (using the word in a sufficiently wide sense to include the Brazilians) maintain, even in this respect, their organic tendency to unity and cohesion. The recent decision of the Brazilian Foreign Minister, Dr. Octávio Mangabeira, that Portuguese be used by Brazilian delegates in every international congress in which Brazil shall take part, shows very clearly how deliberate and conscious is the Brazilian tendency to defend the mother tongue.

But where lapses of translation are easy and terrible is in languages which resemble each other very much, but where words with a similar derivation happen to have a widely different meaning. Thus there can be no doubt that the Italian "meschino" (?) and the Portuguese "mesquinho" have the same derivation — the Latin □. Yet the Italian word means only "little" or "tiny" and the Portuguese word means "mean."

When the languages are still closer, like Spanish & Portuguese, the error is still easier. Sometimes the difference is only of degree, as between the Spanish "escoba" and the Portuguese "escova" (pronounced exactly alike);

the first means broom and the second brush. The Spanish "fecha" means "date," but the Portuguese "fecha" means a □

The minor conflicts of history are all round minor issues, however important these minor issues may be to some of the people involved. The major conflicts are all round great issues — conflicts between religions, between points of view, between civilizations, between cultures.

When, in 1926, the Sebastianist Order established their plan of campaign in Portugal □

6 ☞ Impermanence

[19 — 79]

Impermanence

The problem of the survival of literary works, and of the permanent elements of literature is, after all, a very simple one. All life is adaptation to environment, and all death inadaptation to it.

A work of art is therefore living or great by its approval as [it is] great by a critical environment. There are 3 environments of this kind. One is the immediate one — the nation to which the artist belongs or the strict epoch in which the work appears. The other is the larger environment of the whole course of the civilization to which the nation belongs, in whose language the literary artist wrote, or in which the artist was born (supposing him not a literary artist). The widest environment is that which is not that of a certain nation, nor even of a certain civilization, but of all nations in all times, and of all civilizations in all their eras — that basic human element which is present wherever an organized and cultured society exists, whatever its type of organization may be, of what kind soever its culture.

Certain ideas and forms of sensibility underlie each historical period qua such; certain □ underlie each nation qua such and distinguish it from other nations throughout the space of its allotted life. An art adapted to the first of these environments dies out with its epoch and the small surviving influence of its typical ideas. If these ideas are important or civilizational rather than transitional, the work will make a greater bid for popularity; it will exceed the case we are discussing. An art adapted to a purely national environment, qua national, will only by the shadowy fame of hearsay pass the frontiers of space, and will only pass those of time in proportion as the national instinct it received is near to that basic human instinct which underlies all types of nations and of cultures. That is why Greek art is so rooted in the earth of Time; for ancient Greece was of all nations the one which the most closely conformed to the eternal laws of civilization and of culture. Even if national therefore its art was universal and eternal; since the national and the eternal met in Greece.

[19 — 80]

Impermanence

Some works die because they are of no worth; these, as they die at once, are stillborn. Others have the short day which their expression of a passing mood or fashion of society gives them; these die in infancy. Others, of a larger scope, coexist with a whole era of the country, in whose language they were written, and when that era ceases, they, too, cease; these die at the puberty of fame and have no more than adolescence in the perennial life of glory. Others still, as they express fundamental things of their country's mind, or of the civilization, to which it belongs, last as long as that civilization lasts; these reach the manhood of universal glory. But others, as expressing though with the feelings of one civilization, the language of one country, the thoughts of one era and the style of a passing mood, the eternal substance of the soul of man, outlast the mood, where they drew their style, the age, where they learnt their ideas, the country, in whose speech they are written, the civilization, with whose feelings they speak. These reach that maturity of life which is but as mortal as the Gods, that began but do not end, as Time is; and are subject only to the final mystery which Fate forever veils even from the night that is all around, all between, and chaos that is before and after.

———————

Tricks of style and ingenious turns of mind carry a work as far as infancy. Originality of thought takes it along an age. Depth and splendour of universal feeling make a work go as far as that universal feeling is really universal. Sureness of structure, truth of typical presentation, □ of imagination make a work truly immortal, as far as human things can go, for as near as that may be.

———————

A Kipling is for a passing mood. A Tennyson is for an age. A Spenser is for a civilization. A Milton is for all of time. A Kipling will last for no more than a □ mood, no more at most than a sub-epoch of the nation.

[19 — 81]

Impermanence

Our century is not that of long poems, for the sense of proportion and construction are the qualities that we have not got. Our age is the age of small poems, of short lyrics, of sonnets and of songs. Our survival to succeeding ages will most probably be in the form of *Song-Books*, as those where the troubadours of Provence and the courtly poets of *King Denis' reign* are kept for survival. All that will remain of several ages of our poetry will be (the great names like Dante or Milton excepted) for each nation, a collection of poems like the *Greek Anthology*, finally more an embodiment of a general spirit than the addition of many poems of many individuals — to all intents, save the exact one □, an anonymous publication.

Even poems like *Adonais* will perhaps not survive, because dreams do not. *Prometheus Unbound* shall fade, and in the English Anthology of the future only one or two lyrics from it will speak of Shelley to eternity.

Time deals hastily with those who deal hastily with it. Saturn eats his own children, not only in the sense that he himself consumes what he produces, but also in that he consumes those who are so far his children as to keep their eyes on their age & who work not for an abstract timelessness, the Jovian age of the soul, or the changeless place of that immortal Beauty whom Plato loved.

There is a note of immortality, a music of permanence subtly woven into the substance of some rhythms and the melody of some poems. There is a rhythm of another speech in which the careful ear can detect the note of a god's confidence in his godship.

This note is in the sonnets of Milton, in Lycidas; it is not in Shakespeare's Sonnets, even when they speak of something like it. There is a poise, a calm, a freedom which do not inhabit the fever of inspiration. It is sibyls & prophetesses who are inspired; not the Gods themselves.

The *Moïse* of Vigny, the *Booz Endormi* of Hugo have this note. Of all French poets Vigny is ever close to it, though he attained it not very frequently.

Succeeding times shall have too many poets of ours from which to choose. Too much cannot remain. "Posterity," Faguet said, "likes only concise writers"; true, and a concise number of writers also. Too much is too little.

It is a child's proverb that you cannot eat your cake and have it too; and a biblical one that you cannot serve both God and Mammon. You cannot serve your age and all ages in the same time, nor write for gods and for men the *same* poem.

[19 — 83]

Impermanence

First comes the choice of authors. Gradually, the lesser ones, the derivative ones, will fall back, and the outstanding personalities come to the fore. The works of these, then, shall be themselves sifted, and the natural choice, which took place among authors, shall come to happen to the poems of each author who has survived. An anthology shall be born for each nation — an over-rich, yet no longer a questionable anthology. A final sifting will narrow this to the permanent best.

Thus will the gradual sentence of the ages be passed, and fame narrow down from author to anthology, and from the larger anthology to the smaller one.

For a mind that looks, beyond the externals of the present, to that immortal substance of Beauty which keeps herself shut from what passes, and whose secret is only told to ears closed to the sounds of life and of fame — to a mind like this the unborn trail of the process is simple to foresee. It were a harder, to most extent a useless, though nowise an uninteresting task, to determine, by colour of critical likelihood, which of the authors, past or present, of our civilization can hope for the forum of the men.

Yet if we have ever present those principles which are the embalmers of written beauty, the donors of perennity, and the statuaries of immortal fame, we shall be sure of some books, of some poems, though some others will make us hesitate.

It does not take a very long consideration to perceive the definite immortality of Vigny's *Moïse, La Colère de Samson, La Mort du Loup,* nor of Keats' *Odes to a Nightingale, to a Grecian Urn, to Autumn, to Melancholy.* These poems are as fine as *Lycidas* and shall live when *Venus and Adonis* and *The Rape of Lucrece* shall have gone to human limbo to which all immature beauty is consigned.

The "haunting melody" poets will, of course, die altogether. A "haunting melody" is too ghostly to outlive a short succession of presents.

The principle of *representativeness* will save a few works which the principle of *perfection* cannot of itself let pass. The whole line of boisterous English humour, a unique and deserving thing, will probably survive only in *Pickwick Papers,* which [is] all that Dickens can send in for acceptance to the Gods.

[19 — 84]

Impermanence

It is more difficult to affirm what shall survive by being representative than what shall survive by being perfect, for while perfection has a type and a logic, representativeness exists in direct reference to what is represented, and only in so far as what is represented is important does the representing art survive. But there is the greatest difficulty in knowing what is indeed representative because there is the greatest difficulty in determining what are the important elements to be represented.

Representativeness must be general to hope for survival *on that score*. An artist must *sum up* a *whole age* to live out of that. All secondary and perishing artists represent certain currents; but the artist who survives on this score must represent the current at the bottom of all those currents.

The common characteristic of all the representative artists is that they include all sorts of tendencies and currents.

Saturday night artists

The highest type of this kind of artist is Shakespeare.

Keats is a poet of a higher type than Shakespeare, yet Keats was not greater than Shakespeare. Keats was a creator; Shakespeare was only an interpreter. But Keats ranks relatively low in the ranks of the creators; whereas Shakespeare ranks very high — he ranks first, I believe — in the number of interpreters.

A magnificent type of poet who will survive by representativeness is Walt Whitman. Whitman has all modern times in him, from occultism to engineering, from humanitarian tenderness to the hardness of intellectuality — he has all this in him. He is far more permanent than Schiller or Musset, for instance. He is the medium of Modern Times. His power of expression is as consummate as Shakespeare's. His manner of survival is that of the Rig-Veda and the Bible, representative by plurality of inspiration.

[Representative art: The *Rig-Veda*, the *Bible*. That is: either a multi-personal poet (dramatical, like Shakespeare, or lyrical, like Walt Whitman), or a "collective" poet: the Rig-Veda, or the *Bible*).]

[19 — 85]

Impermanence.

A Greek intellect and a modern sensibility. A Greek intellect because, even if we suppose that a Greek intellect does not mean an eternal intellect, still the Greek discipline of thought is the scientific basis of all our art. A modern sensibility, because we cannot maim our emotions to please the □

Yet our discipline, though Greek in quality, cannot be Greek in quantity. Our sensibility is of [a] complexity which antiquity could not even dream of; so our discipline of that sensibility must involve the use of a far higher quantum of intellectual force.

The Greeks might feel deeply, or strongly or wildly, but they always felt rationally. Their emotions were born reasonable, even where born fiery and violent. Not only can we not attain to that quality, but we must not; for, if we had the Greek intellect & the Greek feeling, we would be ancient Greeks, not modern Europeans.

7 ☞ Uselessness of Criticism

[18 — 42]

USELESSNESS OF CRITICISM.

That good work always comes to the fore is a worthless affirmation if it apply to really good work and by "coming to the fore" it refers to acceptance in its own time. That good work always comes to the fore on the course of its futurity, is true; that second rate good work always comes to the fore in its own age, is also true.

For how is a critic to judge? What are the qualities that make, not the casual, but the competent critic? A knowledge of past art or literature, a taste refined by that knowledge, and an impartial and judicious spirit. Anything less than that is fatal to the true play of the critical faculties. Anything more than that is already creative spirit, and therefore individuality; and individuality means self-centredness, and a certain imperviousness to the work of others.

How competent, however, is the competent critic? Let us suppose a deeply original work of art comes before his eyes. How does he judge it? By comparison with the works of art of the past. If it be original, however, it will depart in something — and the more original the more it will depart — from the works of art of the past. In so far as it does this, it will seem not to conform to the æsthetic canon which the critic finds established in

his mind. And if its originality, instead of lying in a departure from those old standards, lie in a use of them on more severely constructive lines — as Milton used the ancients — will the critic take that bettering to be a bettering, or the use of those standards to be an imitation? Will he rather see the builder than the user of the building materials? Why should he rather do one thing than the better other? Of all elements, constructiveness is the most difficult to determine in a work..............
A fusion of past elements... Will the critic see the fusion or the elements?

Does anyone persuade himself that if *Paradise Lost* were published to-day, or *Hamlet*, or Shakespeare's or Milton's Sonnets, they would be rated above Mr. Kipling's poetry, or Mr. Noyes', or that of any other similarly quotidian gentleman? If anyone persuades himself of that, he is a fool. The expression is short, not sweet, but it is meant only to be true.

On every side we hear the cry that the age needs a great poet. The central hollowness of all modern achievement is a thing rather felt than spoken about.....
If the great poet were to appear, who would be where to notice him? Who can say whether he has not already appeared? The reading public sees in the papers notices of the work of those men whose influence and friendships have made them known, or whose secondariness has made them accepted of the crowd. The great poet may have appeared already; his work will have been noticed in a few "vient-de-paraître" words in some bibliographic summary of a critical paper.

Facsimile of the *Uselessness of Criticism*

[BNP / E3, 18 — 42ʳ: facsimile]

USELESSNESS OF CRITICISM.

That good work always comes to the fore is a worthless
affirmation if it apply to really good work and by "coming to the
fore" it refer to acceptance in its own time. That good work always comes to the fore in the course of its futurity, is true;
that second rate good work always comes to the fore in its own age,
is also true.

For how is a critic to judge? What are the qualities that
make, not the casual but, the competent critic? A knowledge of
past art or literature, a taste refined by that knowledge, and an
impartial and judicious spirit. Anything less than that is fatal
to the true play of the critical faculties. Anything more than that
is already creative spirit, and therefore individuality, and individuality means self-centredness, and a certain imperviousness to
the work of others.
How competent, however, is the competent critic? Let us
suppose a deeply original work of art comes before his eyes. How
does he judge it? By comparison with the works of art of the past.
If it be original, however, it will depart in something - and the
more original the more it will depart - from the works of art of
the past. In so far as it does this, it will seem not to
conform to the aesthetic canon which the critic finds established
in his mind. And if its orginality, instead of lying in a departure from those old standards, lie in a use of them on more severely
constructive lines - as Milton used the ancients - will the critic
take that bettering to be a bettering, or the use of those standards
to be an imitation? Will he rather see the builder than the user
of the building materials? Why should he rather do one thing than
the better other? Of all elements, constructiveness is the most
difficult to determine in a work.............. A fusion of past
elements... will the critic see the fusion or the elements?

Does anyone persuade himself that if "Paradise Lost" were
published to-day, or "Hamlet", or Shakespeare's or Milton's Sonnets,
they would be rated above Mr. Kipling's poetry, or Mr. Noyes', or
that of any other similarly quotidian gentleman? If anyone persuades
himself of that, he is a fool. The expression is hard, not sweet,
but it is meant only to be true.

On every side we hear the cry that the age needs a great
poet. The central hollowness of all modern achievement is a thing
rather felt than spoken about...... If the great poet were to
appear, who would be where to notice him? Who can say whether he
has not already appeared? The reading public sees in the papers
notices of the work of those men whose influence and friendships
have made them known, or whose secondariness has made them accepted
of the crowd. The great poet may have appeared already; his work
will have been noticed in a few "vient-de-paraitre" words in some
bibliographic summary of a critical paper.

8 ☞ Three Pessimists

[14 D — 23]

Three Pessimists.

The three are victims of the romantic illusion, and they
are especially victims because none of them had the
romantic temperament. All three were destined to be
classicists, and, in their manner of writing, Leopardi always was, Vigny almost always, Quental only so in the
perfect cast of his sonnets.[54] The sonnet is non-classi-
cal, however, though, owing to its epigrammatic basis,
it should be so.

All three were thinkers, Quental most of all, for he had
real metaphysical ability, Leopardi afterwards, Vigny

---

54. Giacomo Leopardi (1798–1837) was an Italian poet and essayist of the Romantic period. In Pessoa's Private Library one finds
two books by Leopardi: *Canti Scelti* [CFP, 8–315], and a book
titled *Leopardi*, corresponding to a French translation by Al-
phonse Séché with a selection of poems and prose fragments of
Leopardi's works. — Alfred de Vigny (1797–1863) was a French
Romantic poet. Pessoa's Private Library contains one book
with the *Poèmes* [CFP, 8–558] of Vigny. — Antero de Quental
(1842–1891) was a Portuguese poet and thinker who lived in
the XIX century and belonged to the so-called Generation of
70. His works include not only poetical compositions, but also
philosophical writings.

last, but still far ahead in that respect of the other French romantics, with whom, naturally, he should be compared in that respect.

The romantic illusion consists in taking literally the Greek philosopher's phrase that man is the measure of all things, or sentimentally the basic affirmation of the critical philosophy, that all the world is a concept of ours. These affirmations, harmless to the mind in themselves, are particularly dangerous, and often absurd, when they become dispositions of temperament and not merely concepts of the mind.

The romantic refers everything to himself and is incapable of thinking objectively. What happens to him happens to the universality of things. If he is sad, the world, not only seems but is, wrong.

Suppose a romantic falls in love with a girl of a higher social station, and that his difference in class prevents their marriage, or, perhaps, even love on her side, for social conventions go deep into the soul, as reformers often ignore. The romantic will say, "I cannot have the girl I love because of social conventions; therefore social conventions are bad." The realist, or classicist, would have said, "Fate has been unkind to me in making me fall in love with a girl I cannot have," or: "I have been imprudent in cultivating an impossible love." His love would not be less; his reason would be more. It would never occur to a realist to attack social conventions on the score that they produce such results for him, or individual troubles of any kind. He knows that laws are good or bad generally, that no law can fit every particular case come under it, that the best law will produce terrible injustices in particular cases. But he does not conclude that there should be no law; he concludes only that the people involved in those particular cases have been unlucky.

[14D — 24]

Three Pessimists.

To make realities of our particular feelings and dispositions, to convert our moods into measures of the universe, to believe that, because we want justice or love justice, Nature must necessarily have the same want or the same love, to suppose that because a thing is bad it can be made better without making it worse, these are romantic attitudes, and they define all minds which are incapable of conceiving reality as something outside themselves, infants crying for sublunary moons.

Almost all modern social reform is a romantic concept, an effort to invest reality with our wishes. The degrading concept of the perfectibility of man □

The very pagan concept of the origin of evil proclaims the pagan tendency to be conscious of objective reality. The pagan conceives this world as governed directly by gods, which are men on a larger scale, but, like men, good and evil, or good and evil in turns, who have caprices like men and moods as men have; and governed ultimately by an abstract compelling Fate, under which both gods and men move in logical orbits, but according to a reason which transcends ours, if it do[es] not oppose it. This may be no more than a dream, like all theories, but it does conform to the course and appearance of the world; it does make the existence of evil and injustice an explainable thing. The gods do to us what we do to animals and [to] lesser things.

Compare with this the Christian thesis that the evil in the world is the product of a benevolent and omnipotent God, and the higher logic of the pagan theory will at once be seen. The existence of many gods may or may not satisfy the mind; the existence of erring and sinning gods may or may not satisfy the mind; but the existence of many and erring gods does satisfy the mind in respect of the existence of caprice, evil and injustice in the course of this apparent world.

9 ☞ Writings on the Poem "Antinous"

[14 A — 7–10]

1. We shall discuss, in the first place, the æsthetic problem involved in "Antinous" or, rather, in the denunciation of "Antinous" as immoral. It is said of "Antinous" — as it has been said, from this standpoint, of all artistic works denounced as immoral, and as artistically spoilt by their immorality — that it is a bad poem *because* it is an immoral poem, or, better, than *in so far* as it is an immoral [one] it is a bad (i.e. a worthless) one.

As pointed out in our prefatory considerations, we shall, though at disadvantage to ourselves, simplify the discussion of this point by assuming, with the accusers, that "Antinous" is immoral, though we do not admit that and shall prove that there is good reason for our not admitting it. But here we say "let us suppose that it is immoral." The consequence is that "Antinous" immediately disappears from the scene and we are brought face to face with the generic problem of the relations between art & morality, and the discussion of whether the immorality of a poem affects its æsthetic value. For, since we have decided, in discussing this point, to concede (however unrightly) that "Antinous" is immoral; if it be proved that the immorality of a poem in no way affects its æsthetic value, "Antinous," even if supposed immoral, will escape censure in this respect.

If we have said, in the above paragraph, "any poem" and not "any work of art" it is because the trend of the coming argument will be to establish a distinction between several forms of art, between statues and poems say, in respect to moral values, what is true of the rules to be applied to a poem will be true of the rules to be applied to "Antinous," for "Antinous" is a poem; □

2. Any product of social human activity, be it a statue, a bridge or an election, is susceptible of being discussed under 3 heads — one being the laws of the particular technics, the art or the science, to which it or its □, belongs; the other, the laws of the type of mind which produces it; the third, the social conditions in which, through which or for which it is produced. Thus a statue can, first, be considered from the standpoint of æsthetics; a bridge from the standpoint of engineering, and an election from the standpoint of "practical" politics. A statue, a bridge, and an election, can then be considered psychologically — that is to say, by an analysis of the type of mind which conceived the statue or built the bridge or directed the nation. Lastly, either of the 3 products chosen for examples can be considered from a sociological standpoint.

Our case is with a poem, or, rather, with poems in general. Our case is to analyse scientifically the relations between art and morality in poetry. We have then three successive inquiries to conduct: the æsthetic one, which is, whether the immorality of a poem, objectively considered, in any way affects the beauty of a poem, objectively considered?; the psychologic one, which is, whether the corruption of the moral faculties of the artist does not involve a parallel, co-affected, or □ corruption of his artistic faculties?; and the socio-logic one, which is, whether the inadaptation to social environment presumptively involved in the writing of an immoral poem does — and how far does it if it does — imply or cause an artistic deficiency in the poet?

Yet, all the time, one essential point should not be lost sight of: while we are discussing this problem under the heads of æsthetics, psychology, & sociology, these are *subdivisions* of the problem, they are subordinat-ed to a general *æsthetic* analysis. The *purely* sociologic, the *purely* psychologic discussions of the problem, will come later, in the second and third sections of this book. So, keeping in mind the fact that our investigation is at this moment primarily æsthetic and only subordinately psychological & sociologic, we are at once enabled to simplify a great part of the question.

For, leaving the æsthetic subdivision intact, for it is directly descended from the primary division itself, let us inquire into the questions put as constituting the psychological and the sociological problem, from the æsthetic standpoint.

When, as the psychologic-æsthetic question to be analysed, we say that it is, *whether the immorality of an author affects subjectively his artistic faculties*, we obviously do not refer to works of his into which that immorality does not pass, in which it is not expressed.

That would be a purely psychologic, a purely moral, *no-wise an æsthetic* problem. The relations between the arrant scoundrelism of Salluſt and the *beauty* or *perfection* of his hiſtories, in which that scoundrelism is not expressed, conſtitute a problem purely moral, purely psychologic. For it to become an æsthetic, though ſtill a psychologic, problem, the immorality muſt be objective, that is, muſt be in the book *itself*, not the immorality of the author as man, but of the author as man. So the queſtion becomes: *Do the faculties involved in writing an immoral poem, qua immoral, affect those involved in writing a poem, qua poem, if so, in what or to what extent?* Now the poet who writes the poem is either himself immoral, has the vice or immorality which he has expressed in the poem; or he is not, and has not that vice or immorality. In the firſt case, we muſt ask whether he considers that vice as a good or an evil thing. If he considers it a good thing, not a vice at all, we are again at the case of Salluſt; for □

[14 A — 1–3]

My poem is held to be immoral and the objections to its being immoral are obviously of 3 kinds. Because it is immoral, it is said to be a bad poem, bad æsthetically; the beauty it may have is held to be lessened by its being immoral. Because immoral it is held to be unprintable, pernicious reading, likely to influence to evil. And, laſtly, it is simply held to be bad because immoral, the objection to its immorality being simply & directly its immorality.

I propose to refute these objections severally and in their total — to prove first that even if my poem were immoral and pernicious to reading, that would not matter to its beauty, whatever that may be; to prove, secondly, that, even if it were ugly and immoral, it would not have any pernicious influence at all; to prove, lastly, that it is not immoral at all.

As the tenor of the preceding paragraph sufficiently suggests, I shall, in the whole course of the argument, give the adversary all advantages. Thus, though I shall prove that my poem is not immoral, I shall when proving that its "immorality" in no way affects its æsthetic value, willingly, though angrily, concede to the antagonist that it is immoral & that its influence is pernicious. And, though I shall prove that it is not objectionable as a work of art nor immoral at all, I shall, when refuting the contention that it is an evil influence or has the power to be such, admit, though that is false, that it is possibly objectionable as a work of art and possibly an immoral poem. [Finally, though I shall have by then proved that my poem is neither objectionable as a work of art or as a power to influence, I shall, when examining its morality, leave these points out of the question.]

[Only when, finally, I shall come to prove that the poem is not immoral at all, I cannot concede to the adversary that, though immoral, that matters mostly to its beauty, and, though evil, that matters mostly to its influence; for, as I shall then be proving it to be moral, that cannot be conceded, which, besides being here dispensed, is at issue in the very substance of the question then to be examined.]

[14A — 4–6]

The arguments against my poem are of three kinds — the æsthetic, the moral, and the intellectual or scientific. The æsthetic argument is that my poem is an (æsthetically) bad poem because (or partially because) it is an immoral poem. The moral argument is that it is a poem which is absolutely dangerous and pernicious because conducive to influencing to unnatural vice. The scientific or intellectual argument is that it is an intellectually bad poem because it is based upon a sentiment which is unhealthy and corrupt.

I purpose to demonstrate that if my poem be a bad one it is for æsthetic, not for moral reasons; to do it, I shall have to take up from a new stand point the old problem of the relation of art to morals.

In the discussion of each of the three arguments I shall take up the attitude which places me at the greatest disadvantage, thus defending myself against the maximum attack.

Thus, though I shall demonstrate that my poem is not immoral and that my poem is not unhealthy, I shall (when discussing it from the æsthetic standpoint or inquiring whether its moral side interests its æsthetic one) concede to the adversary that the poem is immoral and that the poem is unhealthy. I shall subsequently show that it is not immoral and that it is not unhealthy. But I shall not use that advantage here.

Similarly, when refuting the thesis that my poem is pernicious reading, I shall concede that it is bad, and I shall concede that it is unhealthy, though I shall have disproved the first part & shall subsequently disprove the second.

Lastly, when showing that my poem is healthy, normal, and sane, I shall not claim for it that it is good (as will have been made clear in the first section) or moral (as will have been demonstrated in the second).

In each case, I repeat, I shall concede the adversary the maximum weapons. I shall argue against his strongest case, though part of it is made of weapons which I have captured or can capture.

10 ☞ Sensationism

Letter to an English Editor

[20 — 86–87]

Sir,

The purpose of this letter is to inquire whether you would be disposed to publish an Anthology of Portuguese "sensationist" poetry. I am aware of how enterprising you are in this case of new "movements" and this emboldens me to make this inquiry.

It is possibly not very easy to explain in such a number of words as may legitimately be contained in a letter, precisely what the movement called sensationism is. I will try, however, to give you some idea of its nature; the extracts which I am enclosing, and which are translations of sensationist poems and parts of poems, will probably fill in the inevitable blanks of this cursory explanation.

First as to derivation. It would be idle to pretend of Sensationism that it comes direct from the Gods or dates only from the souls of its creators, without the human concourse of forerunners or influences. But we do claim for it that it is as original as any human movement — intellectual or other — can be. That it does represent, both fundamentally (in its metaphysical substance) and superficially (in its innovations as to expression) a new species of Weltanschauung, we have no hesitation in claiming. As, I will not say founder, (for these things must never be said), but at least chief responsible for it, I owe it both to myself and to my fellow-sinners to be no more modest over the matter than social usages absolutely require.

As to derivation, then; and the enumeration of our origins will be the first element towards anything like an integral explanation of the movement. We descend from three older movements — French "symbolism," Portuguese transcendentalist pantheism, and the jumble of senseless and contradictory things of which futurism, cubism, and the like are occasional expressions, though, to be exact, we descend more from the spirit than from the letter of these. You know what French symbolism is, and you are of course aware that, being at bottom a carrying to extremes of romantic subjectivism, it is besides a carrying to extremes of romantic liberty of versification. It was further an extremely minute and morbid analysis (resynthetised for the purposes of poetical expression) of sensations. It was a "sensationism" already, though a rudimentary one, in relation to ours. It threw[55] the world out of focus in obedience to those mental states the expression of which would have been incompatible with the normal equilibrium of sensations.

55. through the world our, *in the original document, probably by mistake.*

From French symbolism we derive our fundamental attitude of excessive attention to our sensations, our consequent frequent dealing in ennui, in apathy, in renouncement before the simplest and sanest things of life. This does not characterise all of us, though the morbid & probing analysis of sensations runs through the whole movement.

Now as to the differences. We reject entirely, except occasionally,[56] for purely æsthetical purposes, the religious attitude of the symbolists. God has become for us a word which can conveniently be used for the suggestion of mystery, but which serves no other purpose moral or otherwise — an æsthetic value and no more. Besides this, we reject and abominate the symbolist incapacity for prolonged effort, their inability to write long poems and their vitiated "construction."

Portuguese "transcendentalist pantheism" you do not know. It is a pity, because, though not a long-standing movement, yet it is an original one. Suppose English romanticism had, instead of retrograding to the Tennysonian-Rossetti-Browning level, progressed right onward from Shelley, spiritualising his already spiritualistic pantheism. You would arrive at the conception of Nature (our transcendentalist pantheists are essentially poets of Nature) in which flesh and spirit are entirely mingled in something which transcends both. If you can conceive a William Blake put into the soul

56. occasional, *in the original document.*

of Shelley and writing through that, you will perhaps have a nearer idea of what I mean. This movement has produced two poems which I am bound to hold among the greatest of all time. Neither is a long one. One is the "Ode to Light" of Guerra Junqueiro,[57] the greatest of all Portuguese Poets (he drove Camoens[58] from the first place when he published "Pátria" in 1896 — but "Pátria," which is a lyrical and satirical drama, is not of his transcendental-pantheist phase). The Prayer to Light is probably the greatest metaphysico-poetical achievement since Wordsworth's great "Ode." The other poem, which certainly transcends Browning's "Last Ride Together" as a love-poem, and which belongs to

57. Abílio Guerra Junqueiro (1850–1923) was a Portuguese poet and politician whose work was important to the revolutionary movement that led to the fall of the Portuguese monarchy in 1910 and the establishment of the First Portuguese Republic. In Pessoa's Private Library one finds 11 books with work by Guerra Junqueiro: *Pátria* [CFP, 8–626 LMR], *Oração à Luz* [CFP, 8–288], *Poeira de Paris* [CFP, 8–369], *Oração ao Pão* [CFP, 8–289], *Os Deserdados* [CFP, 8–195], two copies of *A morte de D. João* [CFP, 8–624; CFP, 8–287], two copies of *Os Simples* [CFP, 8–627; CFP, 8–290], *A musa em férias* [CFP, 8–625 LMR], *Finis Patriae* [CFP, 8–286].

58. Luís Vaz de Camões — in English, Camoens — (1524–1580) was a Portuguese lyric and epic poet. His greatest literary achievement was the epic poem *Lusíadas*, based on the discovery of the sea route to India under the command of the explorer Vasco da Gama. Pessoa's Private Library contains one book with the sonnets of Camões: *Sonetos* [CFP, 8–601 MN].

the same metaphysical level of love-emotion, though more religiously pantheistic, is the "Elegy" of Teixeira de Pascoaes,[59] who wrote it in 1905. — To this school of poets we, the "sensationists," owe the fact that in our poetry spirit and matter are interpenetrated and inter-transcended. And we have carried the process further than the originators, though I regret to say that we cannot as yet claim to have produced anything on the level of the two poems I have referred to.

As to our influences from the modern movement which embraces cubism and futurism, it is rather owing to the suggestions we received from them than to the substance of their works properly speaking.

We have intellectualised their processes. The decomposition of the model they realise (because we have been influenced, not by their literature, if they have

59. Teixeira de Pascoaes (1877–1952) was a Portuguese poet, essayist, and philosopher, known as the main figure of the "Saudosimo" movement, which was based on the poetical and philosophical development of the sentiment implicit in the Portuguese word "saudade" (which is considered by the "saudosistas" to be untranslatable, but which bears some resemblances with the meaning of the English words "longing" and "yearning"). Pessoa's Private Library contains 14 volumes with works by Pascoaes: two copies of *As Sombras* [CFP, 8–420; CFP, 8–642], three copies of *Verbo Escuro* [CFP, 8–643; CFP, 8–422; CFP, 8–423], *Cantos Indecisos* [CFP, 8–413], *Marános* [CFP, 8–641], *Terra Prohibida* [CFP, 8–421], *Sempre* [CFP, 8–418], *Senhora da Noite* [CFP, 8–419], *O Pobre Tolo* [CFP, 8–415], *Livro de Memórias* [CFP, 8–8414], two copies of *Regresso ao Paraíso* [CFP, 8–416; CFP, 8–417].

anything resembling literature, but by their pictures), we have carried into what we believe to be the proper sphere of that decomposition — *not things, but our sensations of things.*

Having shown you our origins, and, cursorily, our use of and differences from those origins, I will now more expressly state, as far as that is possible, in a few words, what is the central attitude of Sensationism.

1. The only reality in life is sensation. The only reality in art is consciousness of the sensation.

2. There is no philosophy, no ethics, and no æsthetics even in art, whatever there may be in life. In art there are only sensations and our consciousness of them. Whatever love, joy, pain, may be in life, in art they are only sensations; in themselves, they are worthless to art. God is a sensation of ours (because an idea is a sensation) and in art is used only where the expression of certain sensations — such as reverence, mystery, etc. No artist can believe or disbelieve in God, just as no artist can feel or not-feel love or joy or pain. At the moment he writes he either believes or disbelieves, according to the thought that best enables him to obtain consciousness and give expression to his sensation at that moment. Once that sensation goes, these things become to him, as artist, no more than bodies which the souls of sensations assume to become visible to that inner eye from whose sight he writes down his sensations.

3. Art, fully defined, is the harmonic expression of our consciousness of sensations; that is to say, our sen-

sations must be so expressed that they *create an object which will be a sensation to others.* Art is not, as Bacon said , "man added to Nature"; it is sensation multiplied by consciousness — multiplied, be it well noted.

4. The three principles of art are: (1) every sensation should be expressed to the full, that is, the consciousness of every sensation should be sifted to the bottom; (2) the sensation should be so expressed that it has the possibility of evoking — as a halo round a definite central presentation — the greatest possible number of other sensations; (3) the whole thus produced should have the greatest possible resemblance to an organised being, because that is the condition of vitality. I call these three principles (1) that of Sensation, (2) that of Suggestion, (3) that of Construction. This last, the great principle of the Greeks — whose great philosopher did indeed hold the poem to be 'an animal'[60] — has had very careless handling at modern hands. Romanticism has indisciplined the capacity of constructing which, at least, low classicism had. Shakespeare, with his fatal incapacity to visualise organised wholes, has been a fatal influence in this respect (you will remember that Matthew Arnold's classical instinct guided him to an intuition of this). Milton is still the great Master of Building in poetry. Personally, I confess that I tend ever more and more to put Milton above Shakespeare as a poet. But — I must confess — in so far as I am anything

60. Pessoa is referring to Aristotle's *Poetics*.

(and I try hard not to be the same thing three minutes running, because that is bad æsthetic hygiene) I am a pagan, and I am therefore rather with the pagan artist Milton than with the Christian artist Shakespeare. All this, however, is *passim*, and I hope you will excuse its insertion into this place.

I sometimes hold that a poem — I would also say a painting or a statue, but I do not consider sculpture and painting arts, but only perfected artisans' work — is a person, a living human being, belongs in bodily presence and real fleshly existence, to another world, into which our imagination throws him, his aspect to us, as we read *him* in this world, being no more than the imperfect shadow of that reality of beauty which is divine elsewhere. I hope some Day, after death, I shall meet in their real presences the few children of these I have as yet created and I hope I shall find them beautiful in their dewy immortality. You may perhaps wonder that one who declares himself a pagan should subscribe to these imaginations. I was a pagan, however, two paragraphs above. I am one no longer as I write this. At the end of this letter I hope to be already something else. I carry into practice as far as I can that spiritual disintegration I preach. If I am ever coherent, it is only as an incoherence from incoherence.

Theoretical Fragments on Sensationism

[20 — 114–115]

Sensationism:

Sensationism differs from common literary currents in that it is not exclusive, that is to say, it does not claim for itself the monopoly of right æsthetic feeling. Properly speaking, it does not claim for itself that it is, except in a certain restricted sense, a current or a movement, but only partly an attitude, and partly an addition to all preceding currents.

The position of sensationism is not, as that of common literary movements, like romanticism, symbolism, futurism, and all such, a position analogous to that of a religion, which implicitly excludes other religions. It is precisely analogous to that which theosophy takes up in respect to all religious systems. It is a well-known fact that theosophy claims to be, not a religion, but the fundamental truth that underlies all religious systems alike. As such, theosophy is in opposition, of course, to those parts of religious systems which exclude other systems and also to those parts of religious systems which seem to it to vitiate the fundamental attitude called religious. That is why theosophy, while it does not oppose protestantism as such, opposes it insofar as it is opposed to catholicism; and why it cannot accept such theories as that of eternal penalties, which vitiate, in its opinion, all that is fundamental and true in the sense of the worship of God's creation.

Even such, the position of sensationism is relatively to all artistic movements. It holds, of them all, or of almost all (for we must not allow this term 'artistic movements' to be applicable with a universal generosity to every snake that raises its head above that of others in the literary pitcher of modern confusion) that, in their essence, they are right. Spinoza said that philosophical systems are right in what they affirm and wrong in what they deny. This, the greatest of all pantheistic affirmations, is what sensationism can repeat in relation to æsthetic things. Though supreme perfection (which is unattainable) is only one, yet relative perfection is several. Homer is as perfect in his way as Herrick in his, though the Homeric way is a far superior one. The sensationist admits joyfully both Homer and Herrick to the great brotherhood of Art.

There are three central tenets of sensationism. The first is that art is supremely construction and that the greatest art is that which is able to visualise and create organised wholes, of which the component parts fit *vitally* into their places; the great principle that Aristotle enunciated when he said that a poem was an "animal." The second is that all art being composed of parts, each of those parts must be perfect in itself; as the former was the classic principle of unity and structural perfection, this is the romantic principle of "fine passages" in what it contains of truth, and excluding the error that makes this all, without attending to the higher classical principle, that the whole is greater than the part. The third tenet of sensationism, qua æsthetics, is that, every little fragment which builds up the part of the whole should be perfect in itself; this is the principle which is insisted on by exaggeration by all those artists of which the symbolists are part, who, being temperamentally incapable of creating neither great organised wholes, nor even (as the romantics) large eloquent stretches, put their activity into the eggshell of producing beautiful individual lines, or very short perfect lyrics. That is beautiful indeed, when it is beautiful; but it is dangerous to fall into the impression that that is anything but the lowest part of art.

These are the tenets of sensationism, qua artistic philosophy. That is to say, these are the tenets it upholds in so far as it accepts all systems and schools of art, extracting from each that beauty and that originality which is peculiar to it.

But sensationism is not only a philosophy of art; besides its attitude of universal acceptance of what is beautiful, it presents an originality of its own. If it were only an æsthetic attitude, it would have no right to call itself anything — sensationism for instance —, anything but a bald, though lucid, artistic philosophy.

Qua novelty, sensationism has three other tenets, and it is here that it begins to be sensationism proper.

It holds, first of all, that society is spiritually divided into three classes, which sometimes coincide, & more often do not coincide, with "classes" commonly so-called. It divides those classes into aristocracy, middle class, and the people, but the division, as will be seen, has no relation with the common division of society into these elements. For the sensationist, the aristocrat is the person who lives for art, and for whom all things, material or spiritual, have value only in so far as they have beauty. Religion, morality, spirituality, — all these things are worth the beauty they have, or that can be extracted from them. They are neither true nor false; they have no interest for the aristocrat, apart from their æsthetic interest.

For the middle-class person, in this classification, the basis of interest of anything is political. The value of everything, for him, is in the relation of the political value he sees in it. It does not matter what his idea of politics is; it may be high or low, just as the aristocrat's idea of art and beauty may be high or low, the essential thing being that art is the one important thing to him. So for the middle-class man: politics is the one important thing for him, whether he may be a Herbert Spencer or John Jones, a common voter.

The plebeian attitude involves no direct interest except a material one. All socialists and most anarchists are structurally plebeians, because they are preeminently occupied with economic considerations. The age of economists is the evil age of art, because the age of plebeian feeling must perforce be the evil age for aristocratic sentiment.

Sensationism stands for the æsthetic attitude in all its pagan splendour. It does not stand for any of those foolish things — the æstheticism of Oscar Wilde, or the art for art's sake of other misguided people with a plebeian outlook on life. It can see the loveliness of morals just as it can understand the beauty of the lack of them. No religion is right for it, nor any religion wrong.

A man may traverse all the religious systems of the world in one day, with perfect sincerity and tragic soul-experiences. He must be an aristocrat — in the sense in which we use the word — to be able to do it. I once stated that a cultured and intelligent man has the duty to be an atheist at noon, when the clearness and materiality of the sun eats into all things, and an ultramontane catholic at that precise hour after sunset when the shadows have not yet completed their slow coil round the clear presence of things. Some people thought that this was a joke. But I was only translating into rapid prose (this was written in a newspaper) a common personal experience. Having accustomed myself to have no beliefs and no opinions, lest my æsthetic feeling should be weakened, I grew soon to have no personality at all except an expressive one, I grew to be a mere apt machine for the expression of moods which became so intense that they grew into personalities and made my very soul the mere shell of their casual appearance, even as theosophists say that the malice of nature-spirits sometimes makes them occupy the discarded astral corpses of men and frolic under cover of their shadowy semblances.

This does not mean that every sensationist should have no political opinion; it means that, as artist, he is bound to have none and all. That excuse of Martial's,[61] which has roused the ire of many people alien to the □ of art, ".......... vita proba est," that, though his art was impure, his life was not, reproduced after by Herrick, who wrote of himself: "His muse was jocund, but his life was chaste," is the exact duty of the artist towards himself.

Sincerity is the one great artistic crime. Insincerity is the second greatest. The great artist should never have a really fundamental and sincere opinion about life. But that should give him the capacity to feel sincere, nay, to be absolutely sincere about anything for a certain length of time — that length of time, say, which is necessary for a poem to be conceived & written. It is perhaps necessary to state that it is necessary to be an artist before this can be attempted. It is of no use to try to be an aristocrat when you are a born middle-class man or plebeian.

[88 — 30]

The very curious species of literary movement to which I am going to refer has no direct connection with occultism, but it is not too much to say that every occultist

---

61. Marcus Valerius Martialis (*circa* 38 AD – 104 AD) was a Roman poet, famous for his book of *Epigrams*.

will be interested in it, perhaps all the more interested that the authors to whom I shall allude have not, as far as I know, any occultist intention, though through their works there runs, undoubtedly, the ache of mystery and the terror-stricken feeling of something supernatural.

The brief study I purpose to make will be all the more interesting, I hope, from the fact that the literary movement in question has not, as far as I know, been as yet studied in the pages of any English review or magazine.

The movement in question is the Portuguese "sensationist" current.

It is not my purpose to study the origin of this very recent movement, or determine its relations with French symbolism, with (further back) romanticism, and even, to some extent (more in some works than in others, but not distinctly characteristic of the movement in itself) with futurism & cubism.

The sensationists date back only to 1914, as far as published works are concerned, and to 1909, as I am informed, in point of real beginning of the movement, though it was in 1912 that its leader came to know the other authors who were to take part in the movement. It was brought to a head in the quarterly "Orpheu," [62]

62. *Orpheu* was a Portuguese literary journal that inaugurated the modernist period in Portugal. This journal had only two issues, both published in 1915. Pessoa participated in its first and second issues — with texts written in his own name & in the name of the heteronym Álvaro de Campos — and edited the second issue of *Orpheu* together with his friend Mário de Sá-Carneiro.

two numbers of which have been published, and the third and fourth numbers being said to be soon issued together, owing to the delay of the third number.

Besides the two numbers of this interesting quarterly, the sensationist movement counts only the following works: "Confissão de Lúcio" (Lucio's Confession) 1913, "Dispersão" (12 poems), both by Mário de Sá-Carneiro,[63] "Céu em Fogo" (Burning Sky), eight stories by the same, "Distância" (Distance), poems by Alfredo Pedro Guisado,[64] & "Elogio da Paisagem" (In Praise of Landscapes) by Pedro de Menezes.[65] The last book has just appeared. This is all, and perhaps it would not be quite sufficient, if the kindness of a member of the movement[66] had not made it available to the present author to examine some as yet unprinted poems (by several authors), which contain some of the greatest work as yet done in this new line.

63. Mário de Sá-Carneiro (1890–1916) was a modernist poet and fiction writer and one of Pessoa's closest friends.

64. Afredo Pedro Guisado (1891–1975) was a Portuguese poet from the *Orpheu* generation. Aside from his literary activity, he was also a politician.

65. Pedro de Mezes is a pseudonym of Alfredo Pedro Guisado.

66. moment, *in the original.*

[20 — 103–104]

Sensationism:

I.

There is nothing, no reality, but sensation. Ideas are sensations, but of things not placed in space and sometimes not even in time. Logic, the place of ideas, is another kind of space.

Dreams are sensations with only two dimensions. Ideas are sensations with only one dimension. A line is an idea.

Every sensation (of a solid thing) is a solid body bounded by planes, which are *inner images* (of the nature of dreams — two-dimensioned), bounded themselves by lines (which are *ideas*, of one dimension only). *Sensationism pretends, taking stock of this real reality to realise in art a decomposition of reality into its psychic geometrical elements.*

The end of art is simply to increase human self-consciousness. Its criterion is general (or semi-general) acceptance, sooner or later, for that is the proof that it does tend to increase self-consciousness in men.

The more we decompose and analyse into their psychic elements our sensations, the more we increase our self-consciousness. Art has, then, the duty of becoming increasingly conscious. In the classic age, art developed consciousness on the level of the three dimension sensation — that is, art applied itself to a perfect and clear visioning of reality considered as solid. Hence the Greek mental attitude, which seems so strange to us, of introducing concepts such as that of the sphere into the most abstract abstractions, as in the case of Parmenides, whose idealistic conception of a highly-abstract universe yet admits of a description of it as spherical.

Post-christian art has worked constantly towards the creating of a two-dimension[al] art.

We must create a one-dimension[al] art.

This seems a narrowing of art, and to a certain extent it is.

Cubism, futurism, and kindred schools, are wrong applications of intuitions which are fundamentally right. The wrong lies in the fact that they attempt to solve the problem they suspect on the lines of three-dimension[al] art; their fundamental error lies in that they attribute to sensations an exterior reality, which indeed they have, but not in the sense the futurists & others believe. The futurists are something absurd, like Greeks trying to be modern and analytic.

2

What is the process to be adopted to realise sensationism?

There are several processes — at least three clearly defined ones:

(1) intersectionism: the sensationism that takes stock of the fact that every sensation is really several sensations mixed together.

(2) □
(3) □
How do these three processes realise sensationism? Intersectionism realised it by attempting to realise the deformation which every cubic sensation suffers by the deformation of its planes. Now every cube has six sides: these sides, looked at from the sensationist standpoint, are: the sensation of the exterior object as object, qua object; the sensation of the exterior object qua sensation; the objective ideas associated to this sensation of an object; the subjective ideas associated to this sensation — i.e., the "state of mind" through which the object is seen at the time; the temperament & fundamentally individual mental attitude of the observer; the abstract consciousness behind that individual temperament.

[20 — 102]

Sensationism:

Contents of each sensation:
a) Sensation of the exterior universe.
b) sensation of the object sensed at the time.
c) objective ideas associated therewith.
d) subjective ideas associated therewith (state of mind at the time).
e) the temperament and mental basis of the senser.
f) the abstract phenomenon of consciousness.

Thus each sensation is a cube, which may be considered as set down upon the side representing F, having the side representing A upwards. The other sides are of course B, C, D, and E.

Now this cube may be looked at in three manners:

(1) on one side only, so that none of the others is seen;

(2) with one side of a square held parallel to the eyes, so that two sides of the cube are seen;

(3) with one apex held in front of the eyes, so that three sides are seen.

From an objective standpoint, the Cube of Sensation is composed of:

Ideas = lines

Images (internal) = plans

Images of objects = solids

Looked at in way *1*, the cube of sensations resolves itself to a square, so that the basis of art will be ideas, and images of objects qua mental images. This is classic art, which, contrary to what is thought, does not go directly to nature, but to the mental image thereof.

Looked at in way *2*, the cube of sensations resolves itself □

Facsimile of the Document About the "Contents of each sensation"

[BNP/E3, 20 — 102^r: facsimile]

Sensationism:

Contents of each sensation:

a) Sensation of the exterior universe.
b) sensation of the object sensed at the time.
c) objective ideas associated therewith.
d) subjective ideas associated therewith (state of
        mind at the time).
e) the temperament and mental basis of the senser.
f) the abstract phenomenon of consciousness.

Thus each sensation is a cube, which may be considered
as set down upon the side representing F, having the
side representing A upwards. The other sides are of
course B,C,D and E.

Now this cube may be looked at in three manners:
        (1) on one side only, so that none of the others
is seen;
        (2) with one side of a square held parallel to
the eyes, so that two sides of the cube are seen;
        (3) with the apex held in front of the eyes,so
that three sides are seen

From an objective standpoint, the Cube of Sensation
is composed of:
Ideas = lines
Images (internal) = planes
Images of objects = solids

Looked at in way 1, the cube of sensations resolves
itself to a square, so that the basis of art will be
the ideas,and images of objects, quà mental images.
This is classic art, which, contrary to what is
thought, does not go directly to nature, but to the
mental image thereof. //////
Looked at in way 2, the cube of sensations resolves
itself

[144 X — 49]

Sensationism.

1. As an æsthetical philosophy — Liberal æstheticism.
2. As a social attitude — Higher Paganism.
3. As a national doctrine — creation of national literature.
4. As □
5. As an artistic novelty (else it had no power):

(a) an apotheosis of sensation (this in line with modern ideas — a pantheism gathering into one expression the natural, the artificial, and the mechanic parts of nature, fusing thus *romantic nature-worship*, as carried to an extreme by the Portuguese Saudosists; the cult of the artificial and the false, as pushed to extreme by the decadents who were born, like the Slavic heirs, from the corruption of romanticism, Baudelaire, etc.; and the machine and energy-cult of Verhaeren,[67] Whitman and those propagandist and amusing, though impotent & feeble people, the futurists).

[88 — 41]

Sensationism

After all this attitude is no more than *The Higher Paganism*. (Call it sensationism for advertising purposes, but The Higher Paganism is its real name.)

67. Émile Verhaeren (1855–1916) was a Belgian poet, dramatist, & short story writer, known as one of the forerunners of the Symbolist school.

[20 — 113]

The Portuguese "Sensationists"

A Portuguese once said to me that the worst thing about Portugal was nobody knowing anything about it, not even the Portuguese. The phrase, which is no truer nor falser than such phrases usually are, is singularly right in respect to that curious Portuguese literary movement which its authors have called Sensationism.

Cubism, futurism, and other lesser isms have become well-known and far-talked, because they have originated in the admitted centres of European culture. Sensationism, which is a far more interesting, a far more original and a far more attractive movement than those, remains unknown because it was born far from those centres.

It is, of course, a younger movement than cubism or futurism. Its authors have never tried to make it far-known. But it is due to them to give the movement that publicity they seem, if not to scorn, hardly to desire.

The Sensationists are, first of all, Decadents. They are the direct descendants of the Decadent and Symbolist movements. They claim and preach "absolute indifference to humanity, to religion and to fatherland." They do more and go as far sometimes as to assert that aversion. One of the Sensationists nearly got himself lynched by writing to a Lisbon evening paper an insolent letter congratulating himself with the fact that

Afonso Costa[68] — the most popular Portuguese politician — had fallen off a tramcar and was at the doors of death. There is no reason to assert that any real malevolence lies at the back of statements of this kind; probably they are simply made "to irritate the native" (as the Portuguese say).

[19 — 110, 88 — 31]

The social transformation which has been taking place in Portugal for the last three generations, and which culminated in the establishment of the Republic, has been, as is natural, accompanied by a concomitant transformation in Portuguese literature. The two phenomena have a common origin, in the essential changes which have, with increasing rapidity, been taking place in the very bases of the national consciousness. To attribute the literary change to the political one, or the political one to the literary one would be as erroneous. Both are manifestations of a fundamental transformation which the national consciousness has undergone and is undergoing.

The literary change, represented by the definite rupture with Portuguese literary traditions, can be taken as having a definite beginning with Antero de Quental &

---

68. Afonso Costa (1871–1937) was a Portuguese politician whose political influence was important to the establishment of the First Portuguese Republic. He was also a professor, first at the University of Coimbra and later at the University of Lisbon.

the Coimbra School, though it had necessarily been[69] preceded by hints and attempts at such a change, going back as far as 1770 to the forgotten José Anastácio da Cunha[70] (a greater poet than the over-rated and insupportable Bocage);[71] José Anastácio, with his complex culture (he knew, besides the usual French, English, and German and translated from Shakespeare, Otway and Gessner) represents the first white glimmer of dawn on the horizon of Portuguese literature, for he represents the first attempt to dissolve the hardened shape of traditionalist stupidity by the usual methods of multiplied cultural contacts.

The Romantics continued this work in their half-hearted and lukewarm way; the insufficient power of their action can be measured by the circumstance that the strongest influence they brought into literature was the decadent classicist Castilho,[72] whose damaging sway covers with its leaden influence some thirty years of Portuguese literature, a little recreation of the Dark Ages in modern Portugal, if it had not been for

69. had been necessarily been, *in the original.*

70. José Anastácio da Cunha (1744–1787) was a poet, translator, scientist, and mathematician.

71. Manuel Maria Barbosa du Bocage (1765–1805) was one of the most important poets from the transition between classicism and romanticism in Portugal, commonly classified as a pre-Romantic poet.

72. António Feliciano de Castilho (1800–1875) was a Portuguese writer of the Romantic period.

the parallel existence of real renovating forces, mounting up from Garrett[73] to Guilherme Braga,[74] to Antero de Quental, Guerra Junqueiro (first phase) and Cesário Verde,[75] who was the first to see in Portuguese Poetry, the clearest vision of things and their real presence which can be found in modern literature.

The new introduction of culture contacts took place round 1890 with the bringing in of symbolist and decadent influences through Eugénio de Castro[76] and António Nobre,[77] Guerra Junqueiro (second manner). As the first, it was received with violent disapproval, as every new thing is.

73. João Baptista Silva Leitão de Almeida Garrett (1799–1854) was one of the most important writers from the Portuguese Romantic movement. He wrote several kinds of literary genres from poetry, to romances, articles, essays, plays, and short stories. Pessoa's Private Library contains two books with Garrett's works: *Lyrica* [CFP, 8–211] and *Lyrica I* [CFP, 8–614].

74. Guilherme da Silva Braga (1845–1874) was a Portuguese poet from the late Romantic period. His work is characterized by an obsession with death.

75. José Joaquim Cesário Verde (1855–1986) was the most important Portuguese realist poet of the XIXth century.

76. Eugénio de Castro (1869–1944) was one of the most important figures of symbolism in Portugal. In Pessoa's Private Library one finds Castro's *Poesias Escolhidas* [CFP, 8–98].

77. António Pereira Nobre (1867–1900) was a Portuguese poet whose work was influenced by late Romanticism, Symbolism, and Decadentism. His book *Só* (*Alone*) is considered one of the forerunners of the Saudosist movement in Portugal.

From António Nobre the pantheist movement (which the Porto monthly A Águia represents) gradually worked itself up through Afonso Lopes Vieira[78] (since fallen into imbecility), to António Correia de Oliveira[79] up to the full transcendental pantheism of Teixeira de Pascoaes, one of the greatest of living poets and the greatest lyrical poet Europe now has, if only justice could be done to him. Guerra Junqueiro, as usual, by dint of his extraordinary (and thoroughly Portuguese) adaptability to new circumstance[s], followed this movement also, and the "Oração à Luz," though it has no equal in modern poetry outside Wordsworth's great Ode, cannot however reach the pure flight and wild spirituality of Pascoæs' great Elegia (in *Vida Etérea*).

The central fault of the saudosists, however, was that, what they gained in depth they lost in surface; that while their great merit & originality was gained by a descent (never before realised) into the depths of national consciousness — which the old poets never approached, for Camões is an Italian and Gil Vicente[80] only superficially Portuguese, this of necessity involved a sacrifice

78. Afonso Lopes Vieira (1878–1946) was a Portuguese Saudosist poet.

79. António Correia de Oliveira (1878–1960) was a Saudosist poet influenced by Almeida Garrett's style. He was chosen fifteen times to represent Portugal in the selection of the Nobel Prize.

80. Gil Vicente (*circa* 1465–1536) was the most important dramatist of the Renaissance literary Portuguese period.

of the culture contacts which are indispensable to the essential vitality and greatness of a national literature.

The sensationist movement (represented by the Lisbon quarterly *Orpheu*) represents the final synthesis. It gathers into one organic whole (for a synthesis is not a sum) the several threads of modern movements, extracting honey from all the flowers that have blossomed in the gardens of European fancy. It has gathered into one whole the several movements representing the so-called Decadence, the national movement of which saudosismo is the completion and the more modern currents, of which cubism and futurism are the degenerate expression and which have their remote origin, through Whitman, in no less unexpected a person than William Blake.

The Sensationists have caused □

It has thus added to the fundamental nationalism of the saudosistas the multiplied culture-contacts which the Coimbra School □

[20 — 83]

The romanticists, the Coimbra School and the "Nephelebats" all represent failures in Portuguese literature, in so far as they did not effect (1) a fundamental change in such portions of national consciousness as literary influence can reach and transform, (2) a really coherent body of thought and art conceivable only as Portuguese. That is to say, they did not realise the creation of a national Weltanschauung, as the generally adopted German word defines it. They did not create a definitely Portuguese consciousness of the Universe.

They were bound to fail because they had no ground to work upon. No basis had been given them on which to rear the superstructure of their art. Culture-contacts, abundant and mutually contradictory, are effective in vitalising a nation and a literature when they act upon a national consciousness ready to synthetise them. There is no synthesis where there is no criterion for synthesis; for the same reason that you cannot put things into a box if you have not got the box.

Properly speaking, neither of the movements cited were movements at all. They were merely tendencies, if by tendency we can agree to understand a movement that does not reach realisation. There can be no movement where there is not an element to unify the efforts of a number of individuals, and no number of individuals can be unified without the existence of a national consciousness; they can come together for the reason that they are more or less similar as to temperament, but that association is not durable because it is not deep, and because individual character, though it may bring men together, separates them still more, once they really work out their souls into definite self-expression.

The saudosist movement had to precede the final synthetic movement. The saudosists represent the definite creation of a Portuguese Weltanschauung; the movement will be complete when that Weltanschauung, once obtained and defined, is brought into European activity through the contact with alien cultures. It is this which Sensationism has taken upon itself to do, and its artists have already done much.

The saudosist movement was itself possible only after a succession of culture contacts had so shaken and stirred national consciousness that it had found itself at last.

We are entering on the beginning of the Golden Age of Portuguese literature. Portugal has found itself at last, it is at last beginning to shake off the leaden weight of the anti-nationalist tradition represented by the Italianated Camões, by the Spanish followers, and by the Frenchified idiocy of which Bocage is one of the lamentable representatives. The contact with rich cultures has only served to stir us to a national wakening. But we do not fall into the narrowness of regionalist movements and such like; we must not be confounded with things like the "Celtic Revival" or any Yeats fairy-nonsense. We are not Portuguese writing for Portuguese; we leave that to journalists and political leader-writers. We are Portuguese writing for Europe, for all civilisation; we are nothing as yet, but even what we are now doing will one day be universally known and recognised. We have no fear that it will be otherwise. It cannot be otherwise; we realise sociological conditions the outcome of which is inevitably that.

We work away from Camões, from all the tedious nonsenses of Portuguese tradition, towards the Future.

11 ☞ Fragments on Art and Poetry

[18 — 23–23a]

The aim of art is not to please. Pleasure is here a means — Not: rather many; it is not in this case an end. The aim of art is to elevate. (Proof?)

Before this principle then the famous question of art and morality is quite easy of solution. We do not elevate a thing by making it tend towards evil.

———————

But is not then philosophy an art? Is not the aim of philosophy to elevate also? It is, for knowledge elevates — it cannot lower anyone. My definition of the end of art is then too wide, too extensive. Considering better, then, "the aim of art is [the] elevation of man *by the means of beauty*." "The aim of science is the elevation of man by means of truth." "The aim of education is the elevation of man by means of good."

By this classification we can see how it is that religion means so much; how it is so hard to make men relinquish it. It is that Religion is the practical art.

But I am far from attempting a defence of religion. Indeed it is my hope that we found a religion without God — a religion purely of man, one which has benevolence and kindness as its basis instead of faith *&* belief.

By religion — be it noticed — I do not mean theology. Theology is, if it be anything, a science, forming a part of metaphysics. Theology, being this, is theorical; religion is practical. The creed of Auguste Comte is as more religion than theology — it is perhaps even more, for it has not the egoistic element of a care for self-salvation.

How do we explain the taste of so many authors for subjects which are coarse, unpleasant, repugnant? How are we to explain the □ of Zola; how the "Black Cat" of Edgar Allan Poe?

One reason for this taste is, I believe, to be found, in the scientific and analytic spirit of the author. Another consists in the originality of the subject. Is it in the cultivation of a novelty of sensations?

Is such a taste pathologic or is it not?

Do these poets and the psychologist □

Do they, as Baudelaire in his □, descend

Au fond de l'enfer pour trouver du *nouveau*?

In idealistic compositions the symbol must be vague. By vague, however, I do not mean obscure. Its meaning should be grasped as vague in its limits and in its boundaries — in itself it must be clear. The idealistic symbol must resemble those lofty roman creations of Shelley; the outlines, the *contours* of whose ineffable beauty are indistinct and uncertain.

The satiric symbol, on the other hand, must be clear, quite clear. If it be vague it ceases to be striking.

[19 — 24]

All art is the result of a collaboration between feeling and thought; not only in the sense that reason works, in building the work of art, upon elements which feeling supplies, but also, and it is this that now concerns us, in the sense that the very feeling upon which reason thus works, and which is the matter on which reason puts form, is a special kind of feeling — a feeling in which thought collaborates.

Now thought may collaborate with feeling in three ways. It may be the basis of that feeling; it may interpret that feeling; and it may mix directly with that feeling, so as to intensify it by complexity. The first manner of feeling is that of classical art, the second that of the romanticists, the third that which is peculiar to those artists, who have been described as decadent.

The true classical artist — leaving, as it does not concern us, the discipline and constructive reason he employs, for this is a formal and not a material element — thinks his poem first, and then feels on the basis of that thought. We can find quite near to our times some excellent examples of this: as Alfred de Vigny's "Moise," which is patently an idea worked out through emotion; as Arnold's "Scholar Gipsy," as Francis Thompson's "The Hound of Heaven" (so little classical in anything else except its basis); as Wordsworth's great Ode. It is not necessary to add that all great art is classical, even lyrical; for no art is great if it do[es] not touch our mind at all points, both in feeling and in reason. This no poem does as the classical poem, thus composed. While, in its development it wakes our feeling, it wakes it only that such feeling may give life to the immanent idea which, when the poem is fully read, completely emerges. No great lyrical poem was ever composed except on this reasoned or instinctive scheme.

The real decadent art is that of the romantics. Here the point of departure is feeling; intellect is used to interpret that feeling. Romanticism is nothing else. Hence the intolerable waste stretches of Hugo, where one trite or feeble feeling is drawn out by a subsidiary application of intellect, till the reader is tired; for the underlying sentiment cannot, being trite and vulgar, bear so lengthy a development, and the subsidiary thought (besides its lie to human nature, for intellect, though later in evolution is primary in all the higher life) can do no more than turn round and round the central emptiness of real inspiration. Take, for an instance, Hugo's "Ce que dit la bouche d'ombre": this poem should be about one fifth of its real length, for the central feeling does not admit the rational development, and, as the feeling cannot admit it and yet the rational development is nevertheless made, the result is that most of that rational element is out of touch and □

The system of mixing thought and feeling, though peculiar to decadents, is only really decadent when intellect is used to interpret the interpenetrated feeling; when it is used (as at first seems most decadent) to stimulate that feeling, it is used exactly as in the classicists, save that the artist's intention is not to □

[144X — 49–50]

Society, for us, falls into three divisions. The first, and highest, is concerned with the creation and transformation of intellectual "values"; the second one with the creation and transformation of political values; the third, and lowest, with the creation and transformation of economic values. (So that the first has art, science, and what may be called the sociological part of politics for its sphere; the second has practical politics for the scope of its activity; and the last no more than commercial, industrial, or any other economic, agricultural, etc. each for its own). (There are some readers for whom it is necessary to explain explanations. For those it will be satisfactory that economic and emotional values are put on the level; for, of course, it stands clear, as to the other cases, that intellectual and artistic things are united, and that political and "artistical" things should be the same in this case. But the fact is that the great mass of people, which constitutes this third class, is the one social mass entirely swayed by economic considerations, and the one mass also altogether swayed by emotional ones; not so much, in either case, that they are in this distinct from the other classes, on whom (though, indeed, to a lesser degree) economic and emotional facts react, for they are but human and social, but because they, the mass of the people, possess no elements *to react on those* economic and emotional factors. Every man who lives under the stress of economic necessity is "plebeian" which that stress lasts.

The mental life of those people — "the people" here is understand as explained above — is subordinated in general to three factors: economic, family considerations, & religious ones.

[18 — 48–49]

This problem of immoral art is one that is ever cropping up, centring for the moment round one work or another which puts the vague principles involved in that problem into public focus. There are two aspects to the problem. The first is the abstract philosophical one which consists in the discussion of the relations between art and morals, the æsthetic problem of ethics, if we may so call it, or, putting it the other way, the ethical problem in æsthetics.

I am not now concerned with this problem. My object is to discuss the practical problem based upon these two elements — the problem of pornography, we may say. Should government or any authorities control or supervise the exercise of literary or artistic faculties, having regard to their possibly evil influence on the reading, seeing or hearing public? If so, on what bases will that supervision work?

We will take the problem as concerned with literature. The only classification admissible in literature, which concerns this problem, is into literature proper and mere obscene writing. That obscene writing which is the script-equivalent of, say, obscene photographs, in which the only possible justification is obscenity, belongs palpably to a different species than the writing which is literary and in which either obscene elements are superimposed on the literary substructure, or inextricably interwoven with the artistic substance thereof. So that, if authorities are to interfere in this problem, they have to proceed, first, on a palpably æsthetic basis.

The question, as all questions, is of degrees. There are works which are palpably only obscene and not literary at all, such as those pamphlets, we have just named, which correspond in written manner to the obscene photographs which we also cited in parallel. And there are, at the other end, products like Venus and Adonis, like so many classical poems and prose-works; the difficulty is greatest when we meet with high works of art which are, not only immoral, but frankly apologetic for some species of immorality.

It cannot be claimed that the artistic elements involved absolve and extirpate the immorality of the work. Of the two kinds of public that read, one, the lower, does not see the artistic elements and enters into the significance of only the immoral elements contained in the work of art. The other portion of the reading public, that portion which is sensitive to artistic influences, and able therefore to effect a separation between the two kinds of elements which are, by hypothesis, involved in the kind of artistic work we are discussing, is not very far from the other public in reference to effects, for, if the work be really a high work of art, and the immoral elements therefore not foreign to the substance of it, but inextricably wound up with it, these immoral elements are brought all the more into prominence, inasmuch as they gain intensity, beauty, and fervour through the artistic way they are put.

Venus and Adonis is very likely to excite sexual feelings in a feebly educated person; but it is, if anything, still more likely to excite them in a highly educated or highly-sensitive one. The very artistic superiority of the work ensures that effect. The principle that "to the pure all things are pure" is pure fireworks; there are no "pure [things]."

If we wish to prohibit the sale of immoral art, we cannot do so without prohibiting art at the same time. The problem is especially difficult when we have to consider non-extreme works, that is works which are not palpably superior from the artistic standpoint, but which also are not pure obscenity, mere obscenity and no more. When we are [of] the Shakespeare level, we all more or less agree that it would be tantamount to violence to prohibit the circulation of immoral literature. When we are at the literary level correspondent to the obscene photograph, only the traders in it will not agree to its suppression. But when we are round the popular novelist level, the problem becomes very difficult. To a certain extent works on a literary par with Mr. Hall Caine's or Miss Marie Corelli's are literature; though they are unremaining literature — though several people, indeed, might claim for them a superior level.

If such works convey obscenity or immorality, what is to be done to them?

The central fact is that the problem is elsewhere and its solution rendered impossible until we decide to see that some classification of publics must be entered into, before any light at all breaks into the discussion.

For the essential difference between the uneducated and the educated reading of, say, "Venus and Adonis," is that, though both educated and uneducated are very possibly sensually excited to the same degree while reading the work, the after-influence differs, special cases and morbid ones being, of course, not considered. A little after finishing "Venus and Adonis," the uneducated reader who has not been bored but kept interested by the sexual part of it, remains under the influence of that part of it which interested him, and that is the sexual one. Whereas the educated reader, once past the momentary excitement of the work, remains rather under the influence of the artistic elements.

The second distinction to be effect[ed] is between adult & non-adult public. An adult is held to be one who is able to shift for himself, which a child is not. So that, in this field, the problem becomes simple: the reading of immoral works, of whatever kind they be, should be forbidden to children, but permitted to adults.

Among adults, the distinction follows: there are the educated and the uneducated ones, and the latter are, to a certain extent, in the position of children. So that, if prohibition is to some extent to be decided on, it should be extensive only to the uneducated part of the public.

The question of how that is to be effected is quite secondary & solvable, if only approximately, in several ways.

[18 — 3]

Science describes things as they are; art as they are felt, as they are felt to be.

The essential thing in art is to express; what is expressed does not matter.

[18 — 4]

Poetry is emotion expressed in rhythm through thought. If it were expressed directly it would be music.
Art is self-expression striving to be absolute.

[18 — 57]

A poem is an intellectualized impression, or an idea made emotion, communicated to others by means of a rhythm. This rhythm is double in one, like the concave and convex aspects of the same arc: it is made up of a verbal or musical rhythm and of a visual or image rhythm, which concurs inwardly with it. The translation of a poem should therefore conform absolutely (1) to the idea or emotion which constitutes the poem, (2) to the verbal rhythm in which that idea or emotion is expressed; it should conform relatively to the inner or visual rhythm, keeping to the images themselves when it can, but keeping always to the type of image.

It was on this criterion that I based my translations into Portuguese of Poe's "Annabel Lee" and "Ulalume," which I translated, not because of their great intrinsic worth, but because they were a standing challenge to translators.

[18 — 61]

Essentials of poetry are three: Feeling, Colour, & Form.

Poetical feeling, & to some degree Poetical Colour, may be used in prose; what especially distinguishes poetry is poetical form — Thus in the prose of Carlyle or of Ruskin, or of Jeremy Taylor, there are fine passages of poetry, poetically coloured.

[14¹ — 97]

A writer is either essentially a prose writer, or a poet, or a combination of the two.

The circumstance that an author writes more prose than poetry does not denote him as *essentially* a prose writer and not a poet; it has to be even whatever his type of mind, the essence of his temperament, finds natural expression in poetry or in prose. The definitive proof lies in that inquiry.

How is the mind of the man essentially a proser different from the mind of the man essentially a poet? One consideration will help us to see into this — that all men are naturally rather prose writers than poets. For the normality of man lies in the capacity for adaptation to environment □

Prose is the natural form of literature. Poetry is but a mixed genus — the mixture of the literary and the musical temperaments.

The fact that a temperament naturally seeks poetry, & not prose, for its expression, means that it possesses the faculty of expression in a lesser degree of adaptation to environment.

12 ☞ A Fragment on Translation

[14¹ — 99]

I do not know whether anyone has ever written a History of Translation. It should be [a] long, but a very interesting book. Like a History of Plagiarisms — another possible masterpiece which awaits an actual author — it would brim over with literary lessons. There is a reason why one thing should bring up the other: a translation is only a plagiarism in the author's name. A History of Parodies would complete the series, for a translation is a serious parody in another language. The mental processes involved in translating well are the same as those involved in translating competently. In both cases there is an adaptation to the spirit of the author for a purpose which the author did not have; in one case the purpose is humour, where the author was serious, in the other one language when the author wrote in another. Will anyone one day parody a humorous into a serious poem? It is uncertain. But there can be no doubt that many poems — even many great poems — would gain by being translated into the very language they were written in.

This brings up the problem as to whether it is art or the artist that matters, the individual or the product. If it be the final result that matters and that shall give delight, then we are justified in taking a famous poet's all but perfect poem, and, in the light of the criticism of another age, making it perfect by excision, substitution or addition. Wordsworth's Ode on Immortality is a great poem, but it is far from being a perfect poem. It could be rehandled to advantage.

The only interest in translation is where they are difficult, that is to say, either from one language into a widely different one, or from a very complicated poem though into a closely allied language. There is no fun in translating between, say, Spanish and Portuguese. Any one who can read one language can automatically read the other, so there seems also to be no use in translating. But to translate Shakespeare into one of the Latin languages would be an exhilarating task. I doubt whether it can be done into French; it will be difficult to do into Italian or Spanish; Portuguese, being the most pliant and complex of the Romance languages, could possibly admit the translation.

13 ☞ History of English Literature: Selected Fragments

On William Shakespeare

[19 — 89]

Shakespeare.

Great as his tragedies are, none of them is greater than the tragedy of his own life. The Gods gave him all great gifts but one; the one they gave not was the power to use those great gifts greatly. He stands forth as the greatest example of genius, pure genius, genius immortal and unavailing. His creative power was shattered into a thousand fragments by the stress and oppression of life. It is but the shreds of itself. Disjecta membra, said Carlyle, are what we have of any poet, or of any man. Of no poet or man is this truer than of Shakespeare.

He stands before us, melancholy, witty, at times half insane, never losing his hold on the objective world, ever knowing what he wanted, dreaming ever high purposes and impossible greatnesses, and waking ever to mean ends and low triumphs. This, this was his great experience of life; for there is no great experience of life that is not finally the calm experience of a sordid disillusion.

His wavering purpose; his unsettled will; his violent and fictitious emotions; his great, formless thoughts; his intuition, the greatest that has ever been, seeing right through a thought and expressing it as if the thought itself spoke, living an alien life down to its blood and flesh and speaking from it as the man himself could never have done; his power of observation, gathering a whole thing into one paramount aspect; his practical ability born of his quick understanding of things........

When the higher faculties of the mind are broken, in abeyance, or sluggish in their operation, the lower ones assume an unwonted force. Thus his practical ability was the one thing that withstood the stress and pressure of life and lack of will. He could amass money who strove in vain to amass the completion of created beauty. If we wish to determine whether he was indeed thus, we have to see whether, towards the end of his life, there is not a growth of abruption in practical things.

He began with two long narrative poems — highly imperfect as narrative wholes, and that is the beginning of his secret —, written when he had yet an instinct to write greater than the intellectual impulse for it. With broadening consciousness, he lost his rapidity of □

Facsimile of a Document on *"Shakespeare"*

[BNP/E3, 19 — 89^r: facsimile]

Shakespeare.

    Great as his tragedies are, none of them is greater than the tragedy of his own life. The Gods gave him all great gifts but one; the one they gave not was the power to use those great gifts greatly. He stands forth as the greatest example of genius, pure genius, genius immortal and unavailing. His creative power was shattered into a thousand fragments by the stress and oppression of life. It is but the shreds of itself. Disjecta membra, said Carlyle, are what we have of any poet, or of any man. Of no poet or man is this truer than of Shakespeare.

    He stands before us, melancholy, witty, at times half insane, never losing his hold on the objective world, ver knowing what he wanted, dreaming ever high purposes and impossible greatnesses, and waking ever to mean ends and low triumphs. This, this was his great experience of life; for there is no great experience of life that is not the experience of a disillusion.

    His wavering purpose; his unsettled will; his violent and fictitious emotions; his great, formless though's; his intuition, the greatest that has ever been, seeing right through a thought and expressing it as if the thought itself spoke, living a alien life down to its blood and flesh and speaking from it as the man himself could never have done; his power of observation, gathering a whole thing into one paramount aspect; his practical ability born of his quick understanding of things........

    When the higher faculties of the mind are broken, in abeyance, or sluggish in their operation, the lower ones assume an unwonted force. Thus his practical ability was the one thing that withstood the stress and pressure of life and lack of will. He could amass money who strove in vain to amass the completion of created beauty.

    He began with two long narrative poems - highly imperfect as narrtive wholes, and that is the beginning of his secret -, written when he had yet an instinct to write greater than the intellectual impulse for it. With broadening consciousness, he lost his rapidity of

[19 — 90–94]

Shakespeare.

Shakespeare was initially more vain than proud; at the end of his life — or, at least, of his writing life — he became more proud than vain. It is easy to conjecture why: he was unappreciated; what appreciation he had was more insulting than to be enjoyed, for where he was rated well he was not rated high, and, thinking and knowing himself (for this must have done) the greatest genius of his age, he yet saw how whatever appreciation was shown him bulked small in view of the admiration in which Jonson was held, and others smaller than Jonson, and how appreciation no smaller than shown to him was shown to Daniel, to Webster, who knows if even to the Mundays ("our best plotter"), the Heywoods, & the Days. His vanity was necessarily shaken by this, if not abolished altogether; and the tendency to depression fatal in a temperament of which neurasthenia is a component part must have achieved the transformation.

Pride is the consciousness (right or wrong) of our own worth, vanity the consciousness (right or wrong) of the obviousness of our own worth to others. A man may be proud without being vain, he may be both vain and proud, he may be — for such is human nature — vain without being proud. It is at first sight difficult to understand how we can be conscious of the obviousness of our worth to others, without the consciousness of our worth itself. If human nature were rational, there would be no explanation at all. Yet man lives first an outer, afterwards an inner, life; notion of effect precedes, in the evolution of mind, the notion of the inner cause of effect. Man prefers being rated high for what he is not, to being rated half-high for what he is. This is vanity's working.

As in every man the universal qualities of mankind all exist, in however low a degree of one or another, so all are to some extent proud and to some extent vain.

Pride is, of itself, timid and contractive; vanity bold and expansive. He who is sure (however wrongly) that he will win or conquer, cannot fear. Fear — where it is not a morbid disposition, rooted in neurosis — is no more than want of confidence in ourselves to overcome a danger.

When therefore Shakespeare's vanity gave way to pride, or, better, when the mixture of much vanity and some pride which was initial in him gave way to a mixture of scant vanity and some pride, he was automatically dulled for action, and the neurasthenic element of his character spread like a slow flood over the surface of his hysteria.

The outward intellectual sign of vanity is the tendency to mockery and to the abasement of others. He only can mock and delight in the confusion of others who instinctively feels himself not amenable to similar mockery & abasement. The earlier part of Shakespeare's work is full of "gulls," of derision of some figures. He takes part with some of his creations against others, glories with — — — — — — —

This declined towards the end of his written work. Humour supplanted wit. Humour is no more than the consciousness that what is laughable is akin to ourselves. It is born of the opposite of both vanity and pride, that is to say, of humility, of the sense, rational or instinctive, that at bottom we are no more than other men. Humour, if it had a philosophy, would be deterministic. The effect of the pride he had in checking his vanity, the further checks on that vanity from inappreciation and the insuccess in higher things liberated more & more Shakespeare's humour.

His very pride could not grow because inappreciation dulls pride itself, if pride be not overweening and temperamental, as it was, for instance, in Milton, who, though not very vain, had nevertheless more vanity than he would have liked to have been aware of.

(Let us admire, yet never idolize. And if we must idolize, let us idolize truth only, for it is the only idolatry that cannot corrupt, since what idolatry corrupts is truth, & the idolatry of truth is therefore the only one which stands self-reproduced.)

Only an overweening and temperamental pride can resist constant inappreciation; some doubt must creep into the mind as to whether its sense of its own worth is really valid. The introspective mind has so often seen its Junos turn out to be clouds that it cannot be shaken in the assurance of so naturally misleading a thing as a man's appreciation of himself.

Inappreciation. — There are things in Shakespeare which a lower Elizabethan might have written in a happy moment; these were surely appreciated. But these are the lesser part of Shakespeare; if he had written but them, he would have been a man of talent, of great talent perhaps, not, as he essentially was, a man of genius. In so far as he was, not an Elizabethan poet, but Shakespeare, that is to say, in so far as he was what we now admire him essentially for having been, he is sure to have been unappreciated. Those flashes of intuitive expression which in a cluster of words gather the scents of a thousand springs, those sudden epithets that flash down into the abysses of understanding, these, which are our daily astonishment and the reading over of which cannot pall their novelty nor sear their freshness, must have fallen flat on contemporary minds, for it is in these that Shakespeare, like genius itself, was "above his age." How can an age understand or appreciate what is, by definition, above it? Much of the best he wrote will have been taken for rant, nonsense or madness. We may rest assured that, if we could call up Jonson from the shades and ask him for examples of that want of art and which he charged Shakespeare with, we would be surprised to hear him cite, among things which are perchance rant, many of the jewels of Shakespeare's greater verse.

Yet, as there is an intuition of understanding just as there is one of conception, one as rare & as flash-like as the other, once or twice some of the higher spirits of the age must have caught a sudden glimpse of the transcendency. This would be the worse for the appreciation of the author. Nothing so harms a man in the estimation of others than the sense that he *may* be their better. To the general and constant sense that he is not their superior there is added the occasional suspicion that he may be, & inappreciation, colourless in itself, takes on the hue of envy, for men envy by supposition, who admire only under certainty. Hesitation as to whether a man may be our better is as unnerving as hesitation as to whether something disagreeable may happen to us; we hope not, but we hope uncertainly. And, as we thereby fear the more the event we half-fear, we, in the other case, dislike the more the man we almost admire. In both cases, we dread the possibility of certainty more than the certainty itself ("we know not if we must admire").

Whether it is only the sense of inappreciation that plays like a gloom over the darker tragedies of Shakespeare's maturity it is impossible to ascertain; but it is not likely that such inappreciation should have stood alone in the causation of the melancholy that shows directly in *Hamlet*, that trickles through the phrases of *Othello* and of *King Lear*, that, here & there, twists, as if following the contortion of the suffering mind, the very wording of the supreme expressions of *Antony and Cleopatra*. Inappreciation itself unfolds into several depressive elements. We have first inappreciation itself, secondly the appreciation of lesser men, thirdly the sense that, some effort like that of other men — the learning of one, the connections of another, the chance, whatever it might have been, of a third one, might have conquered the difficulty. But the very genius that causes the initial inappreciation dulls the mind to the activities that could counteract it. The poor and proud man, who knows that he would be less poor if he could but beg or humble himself, suffers no less from his poverty, than, not only from the better status of men less proud or more fortunate, but also from the impossibility of begging as they, or stooping as they to what frees them from a similar poverty. There is then a revolt of the man against his own temperament; doubt sets in towards himself, and, as the poor and proud man may ask himself whether he is not rather unskilled in the things of practice than too proud to descend to them, or whether his pride be not the mask to himself of his incompetence for action, the unappreciated man of genius may fall into doubt whether his inferiority of practical sense is not an inferiority in itself and not only the negative side of a superiority, the defect of a merit which could not exist without that defect.

Shakespeare's case was patently worse. He had stooped to the same arts as the lesser men that stood higher than he, as the still lesser men that stood as high as he or very little below him. He had done the same hackwork as they, without having been worn for that hackwork. He had altered and arranged alien plays, and (whatever he may have thought of that, for it is possible he may have repugned that less than we imagine, being both used to it and integrated in the environment of that activity) he surely cannot have adapted himself to those conditions to the insane extent of thinking he was thereby doing justice to his great genius or in the right place of action for the possibilities of his mind. By doing what lesser men were naturally doing he had become himself, outwardly at least, a lesser man. Not only had he not revealed himself by thus stooping to the common drudgery; he had masked himself the more.

For the learning, which was part of Jonson's credit with the publics, he had, as we have seen, neither appetence nor patience; possibly he even had not time; and he had not received it in early youth, when it is imposed and not sought. From the establishment of influential connections, a humble condition possibly, a lack of disposition certainly, debarred him. To pushing his way among equal, by the social craft of mutual praise and the like □, the pride he had, though not great, was too great, and it would have grown against the attempt, and gathered a fictitious force in the misuse (?).

He had possibly triumphed and made his way materially, in so far as money was concerned. That also, though agreeable in itself — whatever its exact degree might have been —, must have figured as an ironic comment in the margin of his inappreciation. To fail to be known justly as a poet is not compensated by just success as a shopkeeper.

Shakespeare is the greatest failure in literature, and it is perhaps not too much to suppose that he must have been, to a great extent, aware of it. That vigilant mind could not have deceived itself as to this. The tragedy of his unsuccess was but the greater by the mixture with the comedy of his success.

All these are but modes and shapes of the inappreciation which he felt. But the depression of spirit, the dulling of the will, the sickening of purpose, which the sense of inappreciation acting on a temperament like his, caused, must have made themselves felt on other lines than the direct work for which his mind felt itself born. The will which was dulled for writing must have been dulled also for other ways of action. The depression of spirit must have had outlets other than the figure of Hamlet and the phrasing of the greater Tragedies. The sickening of purpose must have discoloured his life, as it paled his poems and his plays. And the joys untasted, the activities uncared for, the tasks avoided and remitted and hurried over must have recoiled, in their mental effect, upon the depression that engendered them, and made greater the dispiritedness which was their cause.[81]

81. *In the left margin of the original document one reads the following handwritten note:* It is almost by this that a Portuguese poet, almost a quasi-sonnet man like Camœns and Blanco White expressed in that sonnet.

To this extent we may justly and confidently go. What else there was, foreign to this, to radicate that depression we cannot now determine; if there were anything. What outward events of an untoward nature can have impinged on that depressed mind, it is useless to try to investigate. Thus much, however, we may say: that those events must have existed. If they had not, the expression of that dispiritedness would have been, not the verbal and psychological content of the Tragedies, but nothing at all. Depression leads to inaction; the writing of plays is, however, action. It may have been born of three things (1) the need to write them — the practical need, we mean; (2) the recuperative power of a temperament not organically only depressed, reacting, in the intervals of depression, against depression itself; (3) the stress of extreme suffering — not depression, but suffering — acting like a lash on the cowering (?) sadness, driving it into expression as into a lair, into objectivity as into an outlet from self, for, as Goethe said, "action consoles of all."

The presence of all three factors can be predicted. The need to write these plays shows in the intensity and bitterness of the phrases that voice depression — not quiet, half-peaceful, somewhat indifferent, as in the *Tempest* patiently written with moderated natural impulse, or on impulsive acceptable, but restless, sombre, dully forceful. Nothing depresses more than the necessity to act when there is no desire to act. — The recuperative power of the temperament, the great boon of Shakespeare's hysteria, shows in the fact that there is no lowering, but a heightening, of his genius. That part of that is due to natural growth, need not, and cannot, be denied. But the overcuriousness of expression, the overintelligence that sometimes even dulls the edge of dramatic intuition (as in Laertes' phrases before mad Ophelia) cannot be explained on that line, because these are not peculiarities of [the] growth of genius, but more natural to its youth than to its virile age. They are patently the effort of the intellect to crush out emotion, to cover depression, to oust preoccupation of distress by preoccupation of thought. — But the lash of outward mischance (no one can now say what, or how [it was] brought about, and to what degree by the man himself) is very evident in the constant choice of abnormal mental states for the basis of these Tragedies. Only the dramatic mind wincing under the strain of outer evil thus projects itself instinctively into figures which must utter wholly the derangement that is partly its own. Depression, if it be inert, is at least calm; when misfortune comes upon it, however, it becomes anguish, and thus, into the stress of the need to react and the scant power to do so, brings the mind near to derangement, when thus our balancing elements, and, when there are not, to derangement itself (Angel and Love's Sonnet).

[19 — 88]

Shakespeare.

The basis of lyrical genius is hysteria. The more pure and narrow the lyrical genius, the clearer the hysteria is, as in the case of Byron & Shelley. But in this case the hysteria is, so to speak, physical; that is why it is clear.

In the lyrical genius of the grade above this — that which ranges over several types of emotion — the hysteria becomes, so to speak, mental; either because, as in Victor Hugo, a violent physical health drives it inwards from physical manifestation, or because, as □
   In the lyrical genius of the highest grade — that which ranges over all types of emotion, incarnating them in persons and so perpetually depersonalizing itself — the hysteria becomes, so to speak, purely intellectual; either because physical health is good but vitality deficient □

— — — — — — — —

   Hysteria takes on different mental forms according to the general temperament with which it happens to coincide. If health be frail in any way, the form of hysteria will be almost physical; and, if the hysteric be a lyric poet, he will sing out of his own emotions, and, the greater number of times, out of a small number of emotions. If health be good or very good, the constitution strong &, except for the hysteria, the nerves fairly sane, the operation of hysteria will be purely mental; and the lyric poet produced will be one who will sing of a variety of emotions without going out of himself — either because, like Goethe, who was of this type, he had a variety of emotions, all, however, personal, or because, like Victor Hugo, he was constantly, though uniformly and monotonously, impersonal and fictitious. If, finally, the constitution be neutral, that is to say, neither strong nor weak, as in the case of a frail but not unhealthy man, the operation of hysteria will become vaguely physical and vaguely mental, neither wholly one thing nor the other; the result will be, in the case of the lyric poet, a mixture of the two others — the capacity to *live* in imagination the mental states of hysteria, the power therefore to project them outwards into separate persons, in other and more precise words, the psychological ability which goes to make, but does not essentially make, the dramatist.

(Shakespeare was then (1) by nature, and in youth and early manhood, a hysteric, (2) later and in full manhood a hystero-neurasthenic, (3) at the end of his life a hystero-neurasthenic in a lesser degree; he was also of a frail constitution and of deficient vitality, but not unhealthy. Thus much we have determined already.)

[14 E — 7]

Shakespeare.

In the highest pathetic flights of Shakespearean tragedy we — those who are accustomed to feel deeply and profoundly — find sometimes lacking, something missing. Part of the pathos is absent. It is evident why. The English race is not capable of attaining the complete depths of feeling and sentiment; in missing those depths Shakespeare is thoroughly English. He is thoroughly English in his matters as in his style.

Over

(To speak truly, in French also we do not find the whole depth of pathos.)

 In English Hood is the one who has gone deepest, in a simple, unambitious manner though — in the "Bridge of Sighs."

———————

On John Milton

[14C — 86–87]

Milton

When, towards the end of ages, Christianity shall have long gone to that vale of darkness where all creeds follow all men, the great power of Milton will stand for it before eternity. When the plays of Shakespeare shall, sunken in forgetfulness be but remembered in a true light of mind as the uncouth sublimities of a barbarous age; when not even the names of the latter poets — as Shelley, as Goethe, as Hugo — shall owe one moment to survival, when the dust of our stired roads shall have settled over the dead bones of those who stired it, this man's songs shall yet sore for eternity before the eternity of the Gods □

His life was given to art, as a thing from him of small price. Every verse he wrote bears the full force of his dedicated will.

Dante and he stand before the ages as reminders of some forgotten thing. The rest is what remains, if that can be said to remain whose very intellect was wit in water, whose fame lived in the shadows, whose influence passed like a bug along despoiled waste, that only took up dead leaves from one place to put those dead leaves in another place.

He was a builder where other men were sand-masons. They made sand-castles on the back of their emotions, more beautiful for the moment; if the end of building were that the thing built should not survive, and that it should be measured by the qualities peculiar to its faults, they were true poets, □

Goethe said once that the function of the artist was *architectonic* in the high degree. No man ever spoke a higher truth, nor lived less by the high truth which he spoke. That he stands condemned out of his own mouth cannot content us, who would rather have stood not condemned.

———————

Only what a man toils to build, does time toil to preserve. The "casual outpourings" of men who have in them all the elements of genius except the dignity of genius.

The very lyrics of a Shelley are no more than occasional verse. All Byron is «vers de société.»

Hugo, though he lacked the sense of perfection, yet, when he forgot that he lacked it, strayed into some perfect poems. Nothing can be more magnificent than *Booz Endormi*; *Á Villequier* falls off that perfection, being too diffuse...

Another thing that is not often considered is that many of the sentiments which we to-day believe to be of all places and of all times, are really only of our time and place. This observation, which might be easily admitted in reference to the poetry of the Symbolists and of the decadents, is perhaps less generally evident when it is brought to bear upon the art of the Romantics. Yet we have no more evidence that the general spirit of man, as manifested critically in relation to us by a distant posterity, will take to Mallarmé as to a poet who keeps, than that it will accept Shelley into its relative immortality. Nothing absolutely warrants the belief that *The Sensitive Plant*, human as it seems to us, is not merely human in *our* age of humanity. What has become of all but the names (?) of the followers of Gongora and of Marini?

All art based upon sensibility rests on an unstable, or, at least, on an unstable basis.

The art which, as the classic art, is based on the intellect stands on a surer basis. Thoughts pass, but not the general structure of thought. It may [be] said that, in a similar manner and for a like reason, feelings pass, but not the fundamental structure of sentiment. Yet this is not so. It is the nature of feeling to have no generality in itself — none until thought shall enter into its composition.

Boileau is safer with the Gods than Shelley. Shelley may, probably is, the greater poet. But if we had to wager on the matter, it should be a risk to back Shelley. Shelley lives on his sensibility, and we cannot determine how far that sensibility is great and human, or how far it is merely *ours*.

Shakespeare survives in virtue of a creative power — the power of creating types and figures. His total incapacity for constructing ordered wholes, his absolute indiscipline of mind, his contempt for all the rules of thought and of art — these things cannot wholly smother the □ vitality of his imagination. But he is not of the Homerics.

Facsimile of the First Page of the Document on "*Milton*"

[BNP / E3, 14C — 86ʳ: facsimile]

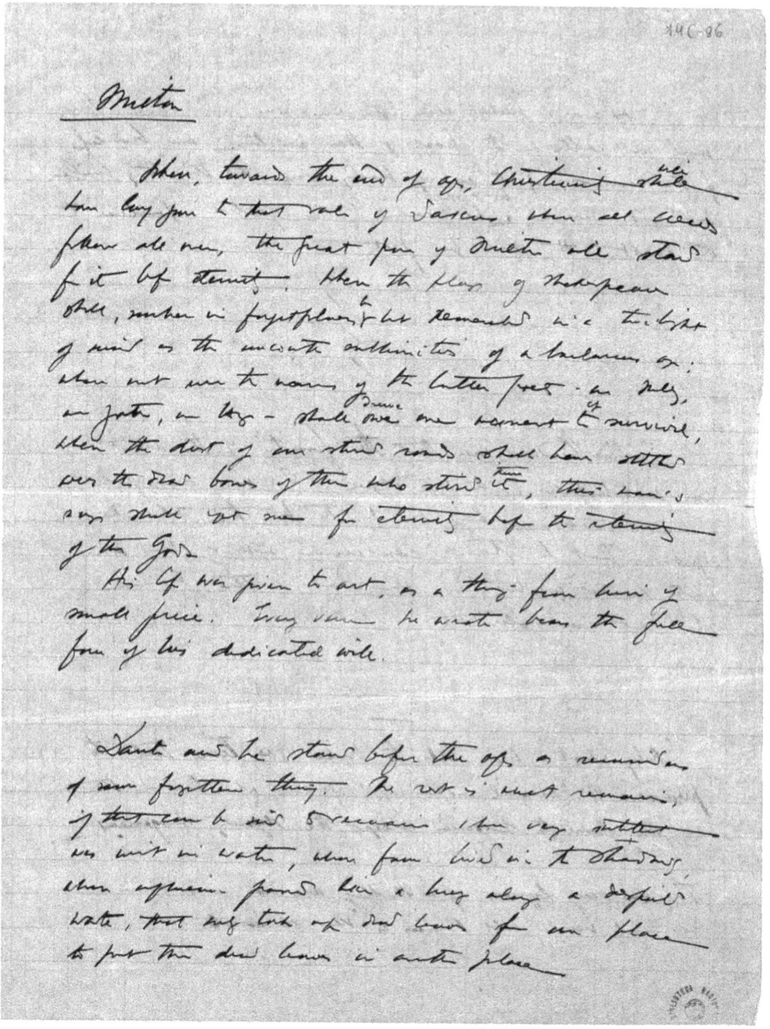
14C-86

Milton

On Robert Burns

[14A — 73]

Burns.

His influence and fame derive from his being a *new thing* in an age yet susceptible of astonishment at anything. — He was bad, but new. He was something to be stared at, Scotch verse was in his case worthless, but there was something new about it, or delicate, its being Scotch verse. The malevolent species that has been uttered on Burns, that the vernacular is all his fame, is to a great extent true, as most malevolent species or Scotches are (find themselves being, *e natura rei*).

No one had ever thought of putting out Scotch verse as English poetry. Burns did that and had a kind of cubist or futurist fame of the colour of astonishment.

Scotch verse is a thing sufficiently astonishing in itself. As a matter of fact, Scotch verse is a paradox, just as scotch measure is a pleonasm. Anybody who does not know what a pleonasm and paradox mean, but knows what Scotch means will at once deduce the meaning of the 2 words he ignores.

[14A – 61]

Presenting thus a narrow novelty, of the kind, though not of the nature of that which Futurismo, or some such movement, presents today, it is natural that Burns should have been celebrated in his times and, by reflex of that great celebrity, in the one or two generations following them. But, in the nature of such fame, he should have lost his position in literature in succeeding generations, and no rational student of fame would have expected him to be cited today on precisely the same level he was coted then. For this maintenance of renown there must be some reason. It is this reason that we shall strive to determine.

It is obvious, in the first place, that Burns owes his celebrity to being considered by the Scots as a "national poet." But why particularly Burns? Other Scots poets, of a genius far greater than □ could be claimed for Burns on any estimate more generous than ours, could represent Scotland just as well.

One important fact is that [a] great part of his poems are written in the vernacular.

The other fact is that he interprets, with admirable accuracy, the lower qualities of the Scots character. The insufferable banality of mind of the ordinary Scot is fully mirrored in his own insupportable triteness and unintelligence. That characteristic, so flagrant in every typical Scot, of uttering the commonest and least with an oracular air and tone, □

That lewdness & alcoholism which are also typical of the Scots □

This explains the "national" fame of Burns, and, indeed, has already been put, with fair justice in a book not wholly just, by the late T.W.H. Crosland. But it does not explain the infliction of Burns' fame on England, and, therefrom, on other nations. England has too many great poets to need to add a worthless Scot to its roll of bards. Other nations, where the suggestion is followed, have no incitement of any sort to receive that suggestion. They derive it, of course, from England. But why is England so hypnotized?

On Percy Shelley

[14 E — 90]

The great fault of Shelley is abundantly shown to us in his poetry — carelessness. His life displays it not less than does his poetry. A man of supreme kindliness in the whole, he yet did things of a truth cruel and incredible from the mere want of close casuistic consideration of circumstances. He was too hearty in his judgments and never perceived how necessary is it to subject the plans, the intentions, and the poetry [of] enthusiasm to a close & impartial discrimination.

[14 E — 89]

Two features of Shelley's character: Childishness and general nature, general abstractiveness of character. A metaphysician, not a psychologist; more warm in his general love of man, than in his affections.

Question: Is this childishness identical with abstractiveness?

On John Keats

[19 — 98]

Keats — I cannot think badly of the man who wrote the Ode to a Nightingale, nor of him who, in that to the Grecian Urn, expressed so human an idea as the heart-rending *untimeness* of beauty. We all have felt that tearful sensation. Mothers, how many of ye, in looking at your bright children and at their heavenly fairness, have not wished such small, lovely forms could be preserved for ever and unchanged. Lover, when looking upon the form of thy mistress, hast thou not felt thy heart oppressed because such beauty should one day be no more, nay, should grow old and, mayhap, unbeautiful. Have we not all wished the immortality of someone that we know, have we all not felt that same pain at feeling that none are immortal. The statue of Roman Venus hath looked, century after century, upon us in its nude beauty, hath charmed generations by its form and liveth now to charm others. But where art thou whom she looked upon? Some faces, fair, perhaps, as her face; some forms, beauteous, perhaps, as her form, where are they now, animated as they were by the fire that she hath not? Apollo Belvedere still stands, but what of the millions of fair youths and maidens that have looked upon him? Their fairness went dwindled to old age, rotted in horrible death, and the uninspired image stands beautiful for ever and ever before us. If we had but each of us an Aurora who would not be content to be a Tithonus, though thin-rocked, would-worn & feeble.

$$[14C — 81]$$

I deem the "Ode to a Nightingale" to be the best of all the odes of Keats, if not in his works the greatest poem. Not that I think it perfect, or that I consider it □, but because a more complete expression of a pained soul, of a wounded poetic spirit, has never been, nor ever will be formulated. Only a poet can grasp the full meaning of this Ode, only one pained and crushed by that blackest of all demons — the material — can catch at the real spirit of this magic utterance, and can point out how great the expression of world-weariness unfolded. Everything in this poem is full of life-spirit, of a pained life-spirit. It is not deep, nor awful, but, to him that can read it, moving to the highest degree. It will ever remain a masterly example of what poetry is.

On Alfred Tennyson

[19 — 98]

Tennyson — "In Memoriam" should be taken as the example of Tennyson's human depth, "Tithonus" and "Oenone" of his half-sensuous perfection, *&* the "Idylls of the King" of his general poetic decadence. The verse of this latter work is in many places abominable; Tennyson's fine music of paragraph is often lost, and at times even his melody of line. Tennyson must not be judged by the "Idylls of the King," or must then be judged unjustly.

On Charles Dickens

[14C — 70]

Does Dickens' attraction consist in the rigour or in the exactness of his character-delineation? In the lucidness of his psychological presentation? In the rigour of his analysis of situations and of mental states? It consists in neither. Dickens is no psychologist, no intuitionist; if ever he sees into thought, it is not the microscope of intellect that aids him but the spectroscope of tenderness. The charm of Dickens is in the atmosphere of kind that envelops his creations. He sees best into souls where psychologists see worst. His characters do not satisfy intellectually, but they do not not-satisfy; this because their manner of satisfying is other. No one asks: Are they correct, exact? Because the manner of satisfaction they give is not this.

Commonplace in thought, trite and vulgar (in no bad sense) in his philosophy, without real dramatic and still less poetic power, he had the genius that springs from kindness, the intelligence that comes of love.

He had not poetic power, but an infinite poetic intelligence. What can be more poetic than kindness, more poetic than tenderness? Nothing; these are at the soul of poetry and he who looks but for beauty & for splendour is an ill poet.

Too much beauty tires. Too much splendour aches. Too much imagination awes and sickens. Too much benevolence neither tires nor aches, neither awes nor sickens. There cannot be too much benevolence. Beauty, splendour, wisdom may come too soon, too late. Love never comes too soon, nor too late, though it always goes too soon.

All who know me are aware how profound an enemy I am to the Christian religion. Yet I were blind and hateful if I were to deny that, though its general influence with the prejudice □ that it gives is bad, nevertheless its central idea, that of altruism, of love, of self-sacrifice, of life-devotion is the greater itself. Could priests and ministers, men who up to now have done much of the evil that hearth has had, but strife their creed of its evil accidents and □; could they bid themselves above all, as the Master bid them to do, not to the "letter that Killeth" but to the "spirit that giveth life."

First Page of the Document
on Charles Dickens

[BNP / E, 14C — 70ʳ: facsimile]

Does Dickens' attraction consist in the vigour or
in the exactness of his character-delineation?
in the lucidness of his psychological presentation?
in the vigour of his analysis of situations & of mental
data? In neither. Dickens is no psychologist,
no intuitionist. if ever he sees it is
not the microscope of intellect that aids him
[but the spectroscope of tenderness]. The charm of
Dickens lies in the atmosphere of kind that
envelops his creations. He sees but into souls
where psychologists see most

Commonplace in thought, vulgar in no
bad sense in his philosophy, without real
dramatic & still less poetic power, he had the
genius that for kindness, the intelligence
that comes of love.

\# His characters do not satisfy intellectually, but
they do but not-satisfy; this ∴ their manner of
satisfying is other. No one asks are they correct, exact?
because the manner of satisfying them is not
this.
He had no poetic power, but an infinite poetic intelligence.
What can be more poetic than kindness, more poetic the
tenderness? there are at the soul of poetry & he
who looks but for but & for splendour is an ill

On Oscar Wilde

[14E — 61–63; 14⁴ — 18–18a]

Oscar Wilde

His attitude towards life was threefold, and threefoldious symbolic. He was a dandy and a specially conscious and complex dandy; he was an utterer of paradoxes; and he was a preacher of self-indulgence and of pleasure, a preacher of these things as a cult.

The peculiar philosophical significance of dandyism has been touched upon deeply by Carlyle, and less so by Jules Lemaître, *passim* in reference to Barbey d'Aurevilly.

The modern phenomenon of paradox is only the thin and felt edge of that body which in its broader breadths takes in pragmatism, intuition, and all those other forms of modern evidentness included scepticism, that is to say, confession of disbelief in logic to explain life and in life to explain logic, in reality to square itself with identity, of social impulses to fall into him with individual tendencies.

He was essentially temporary. He will survive a Johnson, but more literarily graven than Johnson, as a symbolic figure, limited to symbolizing, without anything but the symbolic in him. He has no individuality. His true dictum "most people are other people" stands by its author, descriptively. All Wilde was, as logicians would say, not-Wilde. He had no centre.

Wilde was socially, not superiorly representative, a Johnson not a Voltaire of his time. The three things he was, he was not with that full consciousness of those that could have made him genius indeed. He was a dandy, of real life, not a dandy in literature, except incompletely and by reflexion. He was a paradoxer, but not the strong reason to make his paradoxes, even written, more than momentary: the power to be far-reaching was not in him, as it was not in his opposite analogue Johnson. He was a defender of pleasure and self-indulgence, but neither his work nor his life betray him a whole man in this. He was not strong enough to be really bad or really good; not clear enough to be really logical and coherent or really scattered and □; not independent enough to be either a victor over social forces in himself, or over himself as in opposition to social forces. He was the pure symbolical therefore. Our age is an age of bold cowardice, shallow profundity of thoughts, violent individualism moulded and cross-moulded by string and □ currents of opinion, social movements, snatching up into limitation of individuality self-pleased independent thinking.

The anarchistic character of Wilde is the more anarchistic because it is not completely anarchistic. A thoroughly anarchistic thing — a social state or □ — is immediately suicidal.

Such a man as Wilde could not be loyal; neither could he be disloyal. He had not the character to be loyal, nor the courage to be a real scoundrel. He is representative in this, painfully symbolical.

To represent him as a good & caring man as Mr. Sherard does, is to misunderstand him; to call him a "devil," author of "devils" as Mr. Crosland does, is to misunderstand him. He was neither. He could not be good & dared not be bad. The tragedy of his life is in this.

He was an indifferent poet, a fairly good playwright, and an interesting novelist. I do not think that honesty can speak more praisingly of him.

□ indignations, issued from the shows and the novels of the moral sense □

Everybody knows now that much of anti-aristocratic feeling went into the matter, that there was much more purpleness *in it*.

□ (Quote Sherard — spit) □

The only □ consolation that a decent □ can have is that the same citizen who spat twice in Wilde's face could have (in all coherence) spat ten or twelve in the face of the author of Shakespeare's sonnets.

———————

As a preacher of pleasure, self-indulgence and anarchistic individualism he is especially useful as counter-excess influence to that crushing of the individual of which one manifestation is the growing state-intervention another □

Eugenics

As an utterer of paradox, he is □. He is a pioneer by destruction. Others and greater men — the true men of genius — will build; these destroyers prepare the way.

As *a* dandy he was at least ornamental.

[14E — 65]

I propose to inquire why Oscar Wilde wrote at all. I shall show that, as he rightly thought, he was what is rightly called an aesthete. I shall show that the man rightly called an aesthete does not write. The question will then naturally arise of how it was that Oscar Wilde wrote.[82]

[14E — 67]

The life, the person and the art of Oscar Wilde have already been subjects of many studies and essays. The life is now as well-known as we can expect it to be. The art, as art, has been sufficiently discussed. About the person, however, not so much in itself as in relation to the art, there is, I think, still something new to say. Therein

---

82. *In the sequence of the document, one reads the apparently related sentence separated from the rest of the text by a horizontal line:*

Scary critic bodies which, though they historically exist, are never logically mythical.

lies a problem, and I believe it has not yet been solved. Perhaps I may even say that, though perhaps suspected here & there, it has not yet been even clearly put.

Yet it is not difficult to put it clearly. Wilde was, typically, predominantly or characteristically, what is called an aesthete. He himself thought so, and most have so thought. Now an aesthete is a man who bases the highest interest of his life in the contemplation of beauty, as distinct from the creation of it. His attitude towards life, which is essentially action, and towards art, which is a product, is substantially passive and unproductive. When therefore we find a man who is described as an aesthete to be an active artist, we find what is patently a contradiction in terms. But, as we do find it, we cannot believe it to be a real contradiction. The problem must have some solution. Either we have put it wrongly or the case is a very special one, a departure from some norm. Our solution will lie either in discovering where the problem has been wrongly put, if it so happened, or how that departure from a norm, and what norm, is to be explained.

We shall begin by investigating whether the aesthete has been rightly defined. We shall pass on to investigating whether Wilde was indeed an aesthete. And, as we may have to prove that he was an active artist, since his works are there to prove it, we shall then, if our two investigations are affirmative in their results, have to explain how it is that he was one.

[14E — 68]

Oscar Wilde said that the fact that a man is a poisoner is nothing against his prose. That is right, but it must be understood, on the like setting, that the fact that a man is a money-lender is nothing against his verse.

[14E — 73]

Oscar Wilde

Of all the tawdry & futile adventures in the arts, whose multiplied presence negatively distinguishes modern times, he is one of the greatest figures, because he is true to falsehood. His attitude is the one true one in an age when nothing is true; & it is the true one because consciously not true.

His pose is conscious, whereas all round him there are but conscious poses. He has therefore the advantage of consciousness. He is representative because he is conscious.

All modern art is immoral because all modern art is indisciplined. Wilde is consciously immoral, so he has the intellectual advantage.

He interpreted by theory all that modern art is, and, if his theories sometimes waver and shift, he is representative indeed, for all modern theories are a mixture and a medley seeing that the modern mind is too passive to do strong things.

[14E — 69]

Concerning Oscar Wilde:

......

The central circumstance, of course, is that Oscar Wilde was not an artist. He was another thing: the thing called an "intellectual." It is easy to have proof of the matter, however strange the assertion may seem.

There is not a doubt of the fact that Wilde's great pre-occupation was beauty, that he was, if anything, rather a slave to it, than a mere lover of it. This beauty was especially of a decorative character; indeed, it can hardly be said to be of any character but a decorative one. Even that moral or intellectual beauty which he craves for or admires bears a decorative character. For it is the feelings and the ideas which may be considered as decorative which he loves and indulges in. He makes all other things mental subservient to this outlook upon intellectual beauty. Thoughts, feelings, fancies — these are to him valuable only in so far as they can lend themselves to the decoration and (upholstering) of his inner life.

He loves to describe decorative things and to evoke things decorative.

Now, the curious circumstance about his style is that it is itself, qua style, very little decorated. He has no fine phrases. Very seldom does he strike on a phrase which is æsthetically great, apart from being intellectually striking. He is full of striking phrases, of the kind of thing that inferior people call paradoxes and epigrams. But the "exquisite phrase" of the poets, the poetic phrase proper is a thing in which his works are signally lacking. The sort of thing that Keats produces constantly, that Shelley constantly hits upon, that Shakespeare is master in — the "manner of saying" whereby a man stamps himself as poet and artist, and not merely as a spectator of art — this he lacks, and he lacks it to a degree which is both obvious and unevident; it is obvious because his purely intellectual phrasing is so happy and abundant that the contrasted absence of purely artistic phrasing is very marked, and it is unevident because the pure delight is very marked, and it is unevident because the pure delight caused by that very succession of intellectual felicities has the power to seduce us into believing that we have been reading artistic phrasing.

He loves long descriptions of beautiful decorative things and has long pages in *Dorian Gray* for instance, or in the two dialogues on Criticism, on the subject. Yet he does not evoke these beautiful things by means of phrase that shall place them before our eyes in a living manner; he does but catalogue them with voluptuosity. He describes richly, but not artistically.

His use of the pure melody of words is singularly awkward and primitive. He loves the process but is ever infelicitous in it. He likes strange names of strange beautiful things and rich names of lands and cities; but they become as corpses in his inartistic hands. He cannot write:

From silken Samarcand to cedared Lebanon,

This line of Keats, though not very astonishing, is still above the level of Wilde's achievement. Let us try him on several passages:

$$Q\ Q\ Q\ Q^{83}$$

This kind of failure covers several pages. At the end we are quite weary of it and wish for a breath of art, for some writer, less purely clever perhaps, who may however have the power to catch the utter soul of things.

For the explanation of this weakness of Wilde's is in his very decorative standpoint. The love of decorative beauty generally engenders an incapacity to live the inner life of things, unless, like Keats, the poet has, equally with the love of the decorative, the love of the natural. It is nature and not decoration that educates in art. The best describer of a painting, in words, he that best can make with a painting *une transposition d'art*, rebuilding it into the higher life of words, so as to alter nothing of its beauty, rather recreating it to greater splendour — this best describer is generally a man who began by looking at Nature with seeing eyes. If he began with pictures, he will never be able to describe a picture well. The case of Keats was this. By the study of Nature we learn to observe; by that of art we merely learn to admire.

83. *The letter "Q" repeated several times indicates that Pessoa intended to "Quote" several stretches of text.*

There must be something scientific and precise — precise in a hard & scientific manner — in the artistic vision, that it may be the artistic vision at all.

The defect, however, goes deeper. It belongs to deeper mental deficiencies than to the decorative attitude. Swinburne, who was not a decorative proper, has the same feebleness in artistic phrasing. Here, again, there is the exaggeration of an artistic element — namely rhythm, which nearly reaches insanity in Swinburne. Swinburne was a bad artist because he □

[14E — 64]

Defence of Oscar Wilde[84]

Wilde can be 3 things, if a genius:

(1) a representative man

(2) an uncaracteristic man of genius

(3) a representative genius

_____

Wilde internationally, English & Irishly representative.

His enormous European influence — He a type — absolute selflessness.

_____

84. *Below the indication* "Defence of Oscar Wilde" *one reads an apparently unrelated indication written in Portuguese between horizontal lines:*

_____

A Linda Andorinha

_____

All his life was a lie. That is the beauty and the representativeness of it. He was one of the few men who did not believe even in himself. His interest in himself was an interest in the nearest of his surroundings.

He was not himself. Neither for him anybody else. His soul was peripheric.

Every pose of his was like a secondary cause in the old argument, there is always no life. Every pose of his was pre posed. His consciousness of his pose considered pose.

He became an attitude not a soul.

On Francis Thompson

[14⁴ — 23–24]

Francis Thompson:

I.

The recent publication of Francis Thompson's Work has not only brought into obvious evidence the man himself and the genius of him, but has also rendered possible, for the careful wielder of analysis, a clear perception, at last, of the whither of contemporary poetry. This latter study could, without internal disadvantage, be made through several other poets, and supremely through contemporary Portuguese poetry — so far has it out distanced all European competitors —, but for the English reader no name stands so advantageously in the forefront of opportunity as that of the Paisley poet.

We will begin our analysis by a critical examination of Francis Thompson's work; we will then, ☐

II.

The most important thing, for the ultimate purpose of this study, is to get at the central meaning and soul-significance of Francis Thompson's inspiration. The first misleading circumstance we meet on the way to analysis is the circumstance that he was a Catholic. So he was, but he was not a Catholic poet. Nay Catholic poets are not. I mean this: his vision of the universe, his *Weltanschauung* was such as no really Catholic soul could hold. The manner in which images were found in his mind, the manner in which he thought were unorthodox.

After all, the best manner of obtaining a true glimpse of his soul is to determine his influences. We mean no injury to any appreciation of his genius by naming his influences. Influences are □ that reveal the poet to himself. When they are anything else, they are only copybooks and there is no poet visible.

These influences are:

(1) Shelley
(2) The "Metaphysicals."
(3) William Blake and Victor Hugo.

The first two influences are obvious. Sometimes they are flagrant: (Quote)

William Blake is often noticeable □

And where Blake is, only absence of reading will omit Hugo. Hugo and Blake are alike. This will seem astonishing to many. Yet the *Weltanschauung* of Blake and of Hugo are similar. Their conscious outlook upon the universe is different. But their unconscious, their sense-born view of things, has a similar basis. Further on we will see what that similarity is.

(1) What is Shelley, essentially? What does Shelley, fundamentally, bring to poetry? Only one thing: the spiritualization of Nature. Shelley was the central & culminating point of English Romanticism. And English Romanticism is no more, centrally, than an adoration of Nature rising for intensity in her (the forerunners, Thompson, Cowper) to adoration (Wordsworth, Coleridge) up to divinization (Shelley). The poet who went further in the adoration of Nature was naturally the greatest of all Romantics — and highest adoration in divinization. In Shelley there is a fusion of Nature with Good. In Shelley the sentiment of soul and the sentiment of Nature become one. Hence his thinking in images. And hence his being the first to employ that curious type of imagery that consists in representing the objective by the subjective, such as [he] says of a flower's petals, that they are closed *like thoughts in a dream.*

(2) The Metaphysicals — what did they bring to poetry? This — the sentiment of the interaction of body & soul. Hence the one thing that in them strikes every reader — their complexity.

(3) Victor Hugo brought into poetry this — the humanization of Nature. This is to be carefully distinguished from the spiritualization of it. For the spiritualizer of Nature every thing is valuable spiritually and bodily — it is seen vaguely, its edges are dimmed by perception of the sculpture of it. For the humanizer of Nature, every thing is like a man — *body* and *soul* —

both important. And his vision of it *clear*, he takes in clearly the contours of everything — Hence Shelley and Hugo, both think in images, one has subtle, imperceptible images, like □; the other clear-cut, neat, violently visible images.

And Blake, as Hugo, humanizes Nature (cf. Hugo *Ce que dit*; Blake □); Blake is on no point so insistent as in the importance of minute particulars. (Victor Hugo's influence is not very *clear* in Francis Thompson — because the fundamental influences in him are externally antagonistic to Hugo, Shelley, and the Metaphysicals.)

Hugo seen through Shelley is Blake, □ If you weld Shelley and the Metaphysicals, □

Francis Thompson's defects are clear: (1) his constructive incapacity: neither of his influences is a good master in this respect. Hugo, though not confused, is diffused and lengthy. Shelley is the most within-measures, but only because he was Shelley; the basis of his inspiration does not involve equilibrium — far from it. He, in his genius, had it, but the kind of man he was has it not. (2) There is both confusion and diffuseness in his poetry. His diction is over-involved, his development tortuous and slavish, the total-effect of his poems as wholes is miserable. *He* seems riot. There is no clearness in him anywhere, neither in the detail, nor in the stages, nor in the total poem. Little in the detail, less in the stages, least in the whole structure. Few poems of his stand firm on their structural legs.

He is perhaps a man of genius; he is not very remarkable, though he is often astonishing. There is nothing fundamentally new in him except what is synthetic of former elements. Yet this synthesis is often individual and he is, perhaps, a genius thereby.

$$[14^4 — 15]$$

Francis Thompson:

Shelley thinks *in* images, they *through* images. This is subtle, but can be small-changed. We read Shelley and hardly notice that we are reading images. In the metaphysicals this never happens, not even in their greatest abandonment and self-dispossession. (The modern poet who, though like Shelley always thinks in images, yet thinks in images similarly showing as those of the Metaphysicals is Victor Hugo.)

— At a great intensity of feeling there is a similarity indeed, just as a crystal □ lit from the inside (this is the metaphor for Shelley) and a crystal ball lit strongly from outside shine alike. But the manner-of-lighting is altogether different.

First Page of a Document Titled "*Francis Thompson*"

[BNP/E, 14^4 — 15^r: facsimile]

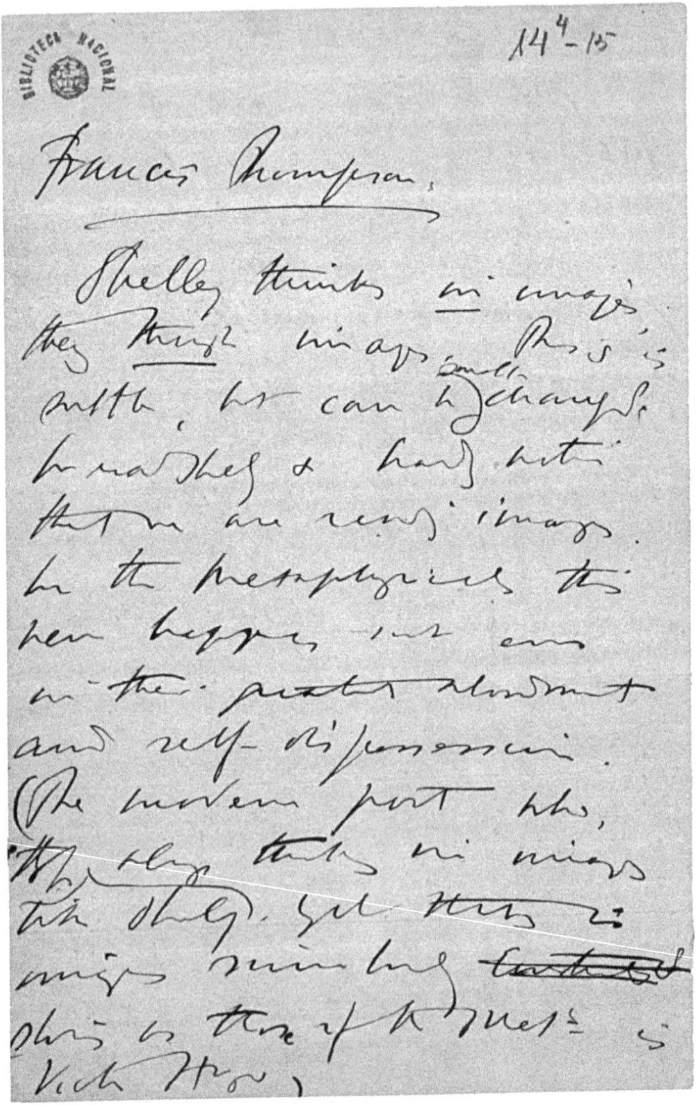

14^4-15

Francis Thompson.

II

Addenda

1 ☞ Other Testimonies Regarding the "Essay on Poetry"

1.1 ☞ Variant Version of the Initial Segment of the "Essay on Poetry" Signed by Professor Trochee

[100 — 2–3]

Essay on Poetry
Written for the edification of would-be
verse-writers
By Professor Trochee.

————

When I consider the superabundance of young men &
the great number of young women in the present century, when I survey the necessary and consequent profusion of reciprocal attachments, when I reflect upon the
exuberance of poetical compositions emanating therefrom, when I bring my mind to bear upon the insanity
and chaotic formation of these effusions, I readily convince myself that by writing an expository essay of the
poetical art I shall be greatly contributing to the emolument of the public.

Having therefore carefully considered the best and
most practical way in which to open such a relevant discussion, I have most wisely concluded that a straightforward statement of the rules □

Facsimile of an *Essay on Poetry*
Version signed by Professor Trochee

[BNP/E3, 100 — 2ʳ–3ʳ: facsimile]

Essay on Poetry.

Written for the edification of would-be
verse-writers.

By Professor Trochee.

When I consider the superabundance of
young men and the great number of young
women in the present century, when I survey
the necessary and consequent profusion of reciprocal attachments, when I reflect upon
the exuberance of poetical compositions emanating therefrom, when I bring my mind to
bear upon the insanity and chaotic formation of these effusions, I readily convince
myself that by writing an expository essay
of the poetical art I shall be greatly contributing to the emolument of the public.

Having therefore carefully considered
the best and most practical way in
which to open such a relevant discussion,
I have most wisely concluded that a
straightforward statement of the rules

1.2 ☞ Manuscript Fragment with the Title "Essay on Poetry" Signed by Professor Jones

[14⁶ — 72ᵛ]

Essay on Poetry

Written for the edification and instruction
of would-be poets.

By Professor Jones

**Facsimile of a Manuscript Fragment with the Title
"Essay on Poetry" signed by Professor Jones**

[BNP/E3, 14⁶ — 72ᵛ: facsimile]

Essay on Poetry

Written for the edification and instruction
of would-be poets.

By Professor Jones

1.3 ☞ Unsigned Manuscript Version of the "Essay on Poetry"

[100 — 10–23]

Essay on Poetry

Written for the edification and for the instruction of would-be poets.

___

When I consider the abundance of young men and the superabundance of young women in the present century, when I survey the necessary and consequent profusion of reciprocal attachments, when I reflect upon the great number of poetical compositions emanating therefrom, when I bring my mind to bear upon the insanity and chaotic formation of these effusions, I am readily convinced that by writing an expository essay of the poetical art I shall be greatly contributing to the emolument of the public.

Having therefore carefully considered the best and most practical way in which to open so relevant a discussion, I have not unwisely concluded that a straightforward statement of the rules of poetry is the manner in which I must present the subject to the reader. I have thought it useless & inappropriate to refer myself too often to the ancient critics on the art, since modern critics are pleasanter to quote & have said all that was to be said on the matter, and a little more — which is their part, where they are original. For putting aside the critics of eld I have two excellent reasons of which the second is that, even if I *did* know anything about them, I should not like to trust my scholarship on the reader. I begin then my exposition.

Firstly I think it proper to bring to the attention of [a] would-be poet a fact which is not usually considered & yet is deserving of consideration. I hope I shall escape universal ridicule if I assert that *theoretically* poetry should be susceptible of scansion. I wish it of course to be understood that I agree with Mr. A. B. in maintaining that strict scansion is not at all necessary for the success nor even for the merit of a poetical composition. And I trust I shall not be deemed exceedingly pedantic if I delve into the storehouse of Time to produce as an authority, some of the works of a certain William Shakespeare or Shaksþere that lived some centuries ago and enjoyed some reputation as a dramatist. This person used to take off, or to add on, one syllable or more in the lines of his numerous productions, and if it be at all allowable in this age of niceness to break the tenets of artistical good sense by imitating some obscure scribbler, I should dare to recommend to the beginner the enjoyment of this kind of poetic licence. Not that I should advise him to *add* any syllables to his lines, but the subtraction of some is often convenient and desirable.

I may as well point out that if, by this very contrivance, the young poet, having taken away some syllables from his poem, proceed on this expedient and take all the remaining syllables out of it; although he might not thus attain to any degree of popularity, he nevertheless would exhibit an extraordinary amount of poetical common-sense.

And I may as well here explain that my method for the formation of the rules, which I am here exposing, is of the best. I observe and consider the writings of modern poets, and I advise the reader to do as I have done. Thus, if I advise the would-be poet to care nothing *in practice* for scansion, it is because I have found this to be a rule and a condition in the poems of today. Nothing but the most careful consideration and the most honest clinging to a standard can be of use to a learner in the art. In all cases I may be relied upon to give the best method and the best rules.

I approach the subject of rhyme with a good deal of trepidation, lest by uttering any remarks which may seem too strictly orthodox, I shall harshly violent one of the most binding regulations of modern poesy. I am obliged to agree with Mr. C. D. when he says that rhyme should not be very evident in any poem, even though it may be called rhymed; and the numerous modern poets who exemplify this precept have my entire approbation. Poetry ought to encourage thought and call for examination; what is then greater than the delight of the close critic when, after a minute dissection of a composition, he perceives, first, that it is poetry & not prose, secondly, after long exertion, that it is rhymed & not blank.

Such poetical niceties, however, being visible only to the experienced critic, the ordinary man of poetical tastes is sometimes, when called upon to criticize a poem, placed in an undesirable situation. For instance, about a week ago a young friend of mine called upon me and asked my opinion of a poem which he had written. He handed me a paper. I made a few, and futile attempts at understanding the effusion, but quickly corrected them by inverting the position of the paper, as better sense could thus be obtained. Being fortunately forewarned that the paper before me contained a poem, I began at once, though without caution, to heap eulogies on the excellent blank verse. Colouring with indignation, my friend pointed out that his composition was rhymed, and, moreover, that it was in what he called the spenserian stanza. Though not a bit convinced by his impudent invention of a name (as if Spenser [85] had ever written poetry!), I continued to examine the composition before me but, getting no nearer to the sense, I contented myself with praising it, and especially commending the originality of the treatment. On handing back the paper to my friend, as he glanced at it to show me something particular, his face suddenly fell & looked puzzled.

85. Spencer, *in the original, probably by mistake for Pessoa writes* "spenserian stanza" in the previous sentence.

"Hang it," said he, "I gave you the wrong paper. This is only my tailor's bill!"

Let the poetical critic take as a lesson this most unhappy episode.

On that bane of poetical feeling, blank verse, I shall only touch lightly; but as several friends of mine have repeatedly asked me for the formula or recipe for its production, I hereby communicate the directions to those of my readers who are so far gone. To tell the truth there is not, in the whole range of poetry, anything easier to produce than blank verse.

The first thing to do is to procure yourself ink, paper and a pen; then write down, in the ordinary commonplace language which you speak (technically called prose) what you wish to say, or, if you be clever, what you think. The next step is to lay hands upon a ruler graduated in inches or in centimetres, and mark off, from your prose effusion, bits about four inches or ten centimetres long: these are the lines of your blank verse composition. In case the four inch line does not divide into the prose effort without remainder, either the addition of a few Alases or Ohs or Ahs, or the introduction of an invocation to the Muses will fill in the required space. This is the modern recipe. Of course I do not know directly that such is the method that modern poets employ. On examining their poems, however, I have found that the *internal evidence* is conclusive, pointing everywhere to such a method of composition.

As to the scansion of your blank verse — never mind it; at first, whatever its kind, the critics will find in it the most outrageous flaws; but if in time you wriggle into poetical greatness, you will find the same gentlemen justify everything you have done, and you will be surprised at the things you symbolised, insinuated, meant.

Before taking leave of this part of my essay, I beg to point out to the reader that in this the age of motorcars and of art for the sake of art, there is no restriction as to the length of a line in poetry. You can write lines of two, three, five, ten, twenty, thirty syllables or more — that is of the least importance; only that when the lines of a poem contain more than a certain number of syllables, that composition is generally said to be written in prose. This difficulty of finding what is the number of syllables that is the limit between poetry and prose makes it modernly impossible well to establish which is one which the other. Internal distinction is of course impossible. After some study I have found that that may generally be considered poetry where every line begins with a capital letter. If the reader can find another distinction I shall be very pleased to hear of it.

First Page of the Unsigned Manuscript
Version of the "Essay on Poetry"

[BNP / E3, 100 — 10ʳ: facsimile]

1.

100-10

Essay on Poetry

Written for the edification and for
the instruction of would-be poets.
—

When I consider the abundance of
young men and the superabundance
of young women in the present
century, when I survey the neces-
ary and consequent profusion of
reciprocal attachments, when I reflect upon the great number of
poetical compositions emanating
therefrom, when I bring my mind
to bear upon the insanity and
chaotic formation of these effusions,
I am readily convinced that by
writing an expository essay of the

1.4 ☞ Unsigned Typescript Fragment of the "Essay on Poetry"

[100 — 7–9]

ESSAY ON POETRY.

WRITTEN FOR THE EDIFICATION AND FOR THE INSTRUCTION OF WOULD-BE POETS.

When I consider the abundance of young men and the superabundance of young women in the present century, when I survey the necessary and consequent profusion of reciprocal attachments, when I reflect upon the great number of poetical compositions emanating therefrom, when I bring my mind to bear upon the insanity and chaotic formation of these effusions, I am readily convinced that by writing an expository essay of the poetical art I shall be greatly contributing to the emolument of the public.

Having therefore carefully considered the best and most practical way in which to open so relevant a discussion, I have not unwisely concluded that a straightforward statement of the rules of poetry is the manner in which I must present the subject to the reader. I have thought it useless and inappropriate to refer myself too often to the ancient critics on the art, since modern critics are pleasanter to quote & have said all that was to be said on the matter, and a little more — which is their part, where they are original. For putting aside the critics of eld I have two very good reasons of which the second is that, even if I *did* know anything about them, I should not like to trust my scholarship on the reader. I begin then my exposition.

Firstly I think it proper to bring to the attention of the would-be poet a fact which is not usually considered and yet is deserving of consideration. I hope I shall escape universal ridicule if I assert that, at least theoretically, poetry should be susceptible of scansion. I wish it of course to be understood that I agree with Mr. A. B. in maintaining that strict scansion is not at all necessary for the success nor even for the merit of a poetical composition. And I trust I shall not be deemed exceedingly pedantic if I delve into the storehouse of Time to produce as an authority some of the works of a certain William Shakespeare or Shakspere, who lived some centuries ago and enjoyed some reputation as a dramatist. This person used to take off, or to add on, one syllable or more in the lines of his numerous productions, and if it be at all allowable in this age of niceness to break the tenets of poetical good-sense by imitating some obscure scribbler, I should dare to recommend to the beginner the enjoyment of this kind of poetic licence. Not that I should advise him to *add* any syllables to his lines, but the subtraction of some is often convenient and desirable. I may as well point out that if, by this very contrivance, the young poet, having taken away some syllables from his poem, proceed on this expedient and take all the remaining syllables out of it, although he might not thus attain to any degree of popularity, he nevertheless would exhibit an extraordinary amount of poetical common-sense.

And I may as well here explain that my method for the formation of the rules which I am here exposing is of the best. I observe and consider the writings of modern poets, and I advise the reader to do as they have done. Thus if I advise the young poet to care nothing in practice for scansion; it is because I have found this to be a rule and a condition in the poems of today. Nothing but the most careful consideration and the most honest clinging to a standard can be of use to a learner in the art. In all cases I may be relied upon to give the best method and the best rules.

I approach the subject of rhyme with a good deal of trepidation, lest by uttering any remarks which may seem too strictly orthodox, I shall harshly violate one of the most binding regulations of modern poesy. I am obliged to agree with Mr. C. D. when he says that rhyme should not be very evident in any poem, even though it may be called rhymed; & the numerous modern poets who exemplify this precept have my entire approbation. Poetry ought to encourage thought and call for examination; what is then greater than the delight of the close critic when, after a minute dissection of a composition, he perceives, first, that it is poetry and not prose, secondly, after long exertion, that it is rhymed & not blank.

Such poetical niceties, however, being visible only to the experienced critic, the ordinary man of poetical tastes is sometimes, when called upon to criticize a poem, placed in an undesirable situation. For instance, about a week ago a young friend of mine called upon me and asked my opinion of a poem which he had written. He handed me a paper. I made a few, and futile attempts at understanding the effusion, but quickly corrected them by inverting the position of the paper, as better sense could thus be obtained. Being fortunately forewarned that the paper before me contained a poem, I began at once, though without caution, to heap eulogies on the excellent blank verse. Colouring with indignation, my friend pointed out that his composition □

First Page of the Unsigned Typescript Fragment of the "Essay on Poetry"

[BNP/E3, 100 — 7ʳ: facsimile]

ESSAY ON POETRY .

WRITTEN FOR THE EDIFICATION AND FOR THE INSTRUCTION
OF WOULD-BE POETS.

When I consider the abundance of young men and the
superabundance of young women in the present century, when I
survey the necessary and consequent profusion of reciprocal attachments, when I reflect upon the great number of poetical compositions emanating therefrom, when I bring my mind to bear upon
the insanity and chaotic formation of these effusions, I am
readily convinced that by writing an expository essay of the
poetical art I shall be greatly contributing to the emolument
of the public.

Having therefore carefully considered the best and most
practical way in which to open so relevant a discussion, I have
not unwisely concluded that a straightforward statement of the
rules of poetry is the manner in which I must present the subject to the reader. I have thought it useless and inappropriate
to refer myself too often to the ancient critics on the art,
since modern critics are pleasanter to quote and have said all
that was to be said on the matter, and a little more - which is
their part, where they are original. For putting aside the critics of old I have two very good reasons of which the second is
that, even if I did know anything about them, I should not like
to thrust my scholarship on the reader. I begin then my exposition.

Firstly I think it proper to bring to the attention of

./.

2 ☞ "Antinous": A Poem by Fernando Pessoa

["Antinous," In: *English Poems I–II*, Lisbon, Olisipo, 1921, pp. 5–16]

ANTINOUS

The rain outside was cold in Hadrian's soul.

The boy lay dead
On the low couch, on whose denuded whole,
To Hadrian's eyes, whose sorrow was a dread,
The shadowy light of Death's eclipse was shed.

The boy lay dead, and the day seemed a night
Outside. The rain fell like a sick affright
Of Nature at her work in killing him.
Memory of what he was gave no delight,
Delight at what he was was dead and dim.

O hands that once had clasped Hadrian's warm hands,
Whose cold now found them cold!
O hair bound erstwhile with the pressing bands!
O eyes half-diffidently bold!
O bare female male-body such
As a god's likeness to humanity!
O lips whose opening redness erst could touch

155

Lust's seats with a live art's variety!
O fingers skilled in things not to be told!
O tongue which, counter-tongued, made the blood bold!
O complete regency of lust throned on
Raged consciousness's spilled suspension!
These things are things that now must be no more.
The rain is silent, and the Emperor
Sinks by the couch. His grief is like a rage,
For the gods take away the life they give
And spoil the beauty they made live.
He weeps and knows that every future age
Is looking on him out of the to-be;
His love is on a universal stage;
A thousand unborn eyes weep with his misery.

Antinous is dead, is dead for ever,
Is dead for ever and all loves lament.
Venus herself, that was Adonis' lover,
Seeing him, that newly lived, now dead again,
Lends her old grief's renewal to be blent
With Hadrian's pain.

Now is Apollo sad because the stealer
Of his white body is for ever cold.
No careful kisses on that nippled point
Covering his heart-beats' silent place restore
His life again to ope his eyes and feel her
Presence along his veins Love's fortress hold.

No warmth of his another's warmth demands.
Now will his hands behind his head no more
Linked, in that posture giving all but hands,
On the projected body hands implore.

The rain falls, and he lies like one who hath
Forgotten all the gestures of his love
And lies awake waiting their hot return.
But all his arts and toys are now with Death.
This human ice no way of heat can move;
These ashes of a fire no flame can burn.

O Hadrian, what will now thy cold life be?
What boots it to be lord of men and might?
His absence o' er thy visible empery
Comes like a night,
Nor is there morn in hopes of new delight.
Now are thy nights widowed of love and kisses;
Now are thy days robbed of the night's awaiting;
Now have thy lips no purpose for thy blisses,
Left but to speak the name that Death is mating
With solitude and sorrow and affright.

Thy vague hands grope, as if they had dropped joy.
To hear that the rain ceases lift thy head,
And thy raised glance take to the lovely boy.
Naked he lies upon that memoried bed;
By thine own hand he lies uncoverèd.
There was he wont thy dangling sense to cloy,

And uncloy with more cloying, and annoy
With newer uncloying till thy senses bled.

His hand and mouth knew games to reinstal
Desire that thy worn spine was hurt to follow.
Sometimes it seemed to thee that all was hollow
In sense in each new straining of sucked lust.
Then still new turns of toying would he call
To thy nerves' flesh, and thou wouldst tremble and fall
Back on thy cushions with thy mind's sense hushed.

«Beautiful was my love, yet melancholy.
He had that art, that makes love captive wholly,
Of being slowly sad among lust's rages.
Now the Nile gave him up, the eternal Nile.
Under his wet locks Death's blue paleness wages
Now war upon our wishing with sad smile.»

Even as he thinks, the lust that is no more
Than a memory of lust revives and takes
His senses by the hand, his felt flesh wakes,
And all becomes again what 'twas before.
The dead body on the bed starts up and lives
And comes to lie with him, close, closer, and
A creeping love-wise and invisible hand
At every body-entrance to his lust
Whispers caresses which flit off yet just
Remain enough to bleed his last nerve's strand,
O sweet and cruel Parthian fugitives!

So he half rises, looking on his lover,
That now can love nothing but what none know.
Vaguely, half-seeing what he doth behold,
He runs his cold lips all the body over.
And so ice-senseless are his lips that, lo!,
He scarce tastes death from the dead body's cold,
But it seems both are dead or living both
And love is still the presence and the mover.
Then his lips cease on the other lips' cold sloth.

Ah, there the wanting breath reminds his lips
That from beyond the gods hath moved a mist
Between him and this boy. His finger-tips,
Still idly searching o'er the body, list
For some flesh-response to their waking mood.
But their love-question is not understood:
The god is dead whose cult was to be kissed!

He lifts his hand up to where heaven should be
And cries on the mute gods to know his pain.
Let your calm faces turn aside to his plea,
O granting powers! He will yield up his reign.
In the still deserts he will parchèd live,
In the far barbarous roads beggar or slave,
But to his arms again the warm boy give!
Forego that space ye meant to be his grave!

Take all the female loveliness of earth
And in one mound of death its remnant spill!

But, by sweet Ganymede, that Jove found worth
And above Hebe did elect to fill
His cup at his high feasting, and instil
The friendlier love that fills the other's dearth,
The clod of female embraces resolve
To dust, O father of the gods, but spare
This boy and his white body and golden hair!
Maybe thy better Ganymede thou feel'st
That he should be, and out of jealous care
From Hadrian's arms to thine his beauty steal'st.

He was a kitten playing with lust, playing
With his own and with Hadrian's, sometimes one
And sometimes two, now linking now undone;
Now leaving lust, now lust's high lusts delaying;
Now eyeing lust not wide, but from askance
Jumping round on lust's half-unexpectance;
Now softly gripping, then with fury holding,
Now playfully playing, now seriously, now lying
By th' side of lust looking at it, now spying
Which way to take lust in his lust's withholding.

Thus did the hours slide from their tangled hands
And from their mixèd limbs the moments slip.
Now were his arms dead leaves, now iron bands;
Now were his lips cups, now the things that sip;
Now were his eyes too closed and now too looking;
Now were his uncontinuings frenzy working;
Now were his arts a feather and now a whip.

That love they lived as a religion
Offered to gods that come themselves to men.
Sometimes he was adorned or made to don
Half-vestures, then in statued nudity
Did imitate some god that seems to be
By marble's accurate virtue men's again.
Now was he Venus, white out of the seas;
And now was he Apollo, young and golden;
Now as Jove sate he in mock judgment over
The presence at his feet of his slaved lover;
Now was he an acted rite, by one beholden,
In ever-repositioned mysteries.

Now he is something anyone can be.
O stark negation of the thing it is!
O golden-haired moon-cold loveliness!
Too cold! too cold! and love as cold as he!
Love through the memories of his love doth roam
As through a labyrinth, in sad madness glad,
And now calls on his name and bids him come,
And now is smiling at his imaged coming
That is i'th' heart like faces in the gloaming —
Mere shining shadows of the forms they had.

The rain again like a vague pain arose
And put the sense of wetness in the air.
Suddenly did the Emperor suppose
He saw this room and all in it from far.
He saw the couch, the boy, and his own frame

Cast down against the couch, and he became
A clearer presence to himself, and said
These words unuttered, save to his soul's dread:

«I shall build thee a statue that will be
To the continued future evidence
Of my love and thy beauty and the sense
That beauty giveth of divinity.
Though death with subtle uncovering hands remove
The apparel of life and empire from our love,
Yet its nude statue, that thou dost inspirit,
All future times, whether they will't or not,
Shall, like a gift a forcing god hath brought,
Inevitably inherit.

«Ay, this thy statue shall I build, and set
Upon the pinnacle of being thine, that Time
By its subtle dim crime
Will fear to eat it from life, or to fret
With war's or envy's rage from bulk and stone.
Fate cannot be that! Gods themselves, that make
Things change, Fate's own hand, that doth overtake
The gods themselves with darkness, will draw back
From marring thus thy statue and my boon,
Leaving the wide world hollow with thy lack.

«This picture of our love will bridge the ages.
It will loom white out of the past and be
Eternal, like a Roman victory,

In every heart the future will give rages
Of not being our love's contemporary.

«Yet oh that this were needed not, and thou
Wert the red flower perfuming my life,
The garland on the brows of my delight,
The living flame on altars of my soul!
Would all this were a thing thou mightest now
Smile at from under thy death-mocking lids
And wonder that I should so put a strife
Twixt me and gods for thy lost presence bright;
Were there nought in this but my empty dole
And thy awakening smile half to condole
With what my dreaming pain to hope forbids.»

Thus went he, like a lover who is waiting,
From place to place in his dim doubting mind.
Now was his hope a great intention fating
Its wish to being, now felt he he was blind
In some point of his seen wish undefined.

When love meets death we know not what to feel.
When death foils love we know not what to know.
Now did his doubt hope, now did his hope doubt;
Now what his wish dreamed the dream's sense did flout
And to a sullen emptiness congeal.
Then again the gods fanned love's darkening glow.

«Thy death has given me a higher lust —
A flesh-lust raging for eternity.
On mine imperial fate I set my trust
That the high gods, that made me emperor be,
Will not annul from a more real life
My wish that thou should'st live for e'er and stand
A fleshly presence on their better land,
More lovely yet not lovelier, for there
No things impossible our wishes mar
Nor pain our hearts with change and time and strife.

«Love, love, my love! thou art already a god.
This thought of mine, which I a wish believe,
Is no wish, but a sight, to me allowed
By the great gods, that love love and can give
To mortal hearts, under the shape of wishes —
Of wishes having undiscovered reaches —,
A vision of the real things beyond
Our life-imprisoned life, our sense-bound sense.
Ay, what I wish thee to be thou art now
Already. Already on Olympic ground
Thou walkest and art perfect, yet art thou,
For thou needst no excess of thee to don
Perfect to be, being perfection.

«My heart is singing like a morning bird.
A great hope from the gods comes down to me
And bids my heart to subtler sense be stirred
And think not that strange evil of thee
That to think thee mortal would be.

«My love, my love, my god-love! Let me kiss
On thy cold lips thy hot lips now immortal,
Greeting thee at Death's portal's happiness,
For to the gods Death's portal is Life's portal.

«Were no Olympus yet for thee, my love
Would make thee one, where thou sole god mightst prove,
And I thy sole adorer, glad to be
Thy sole adorer through infinity.
That were a universe divine enough
For love and me and what to me thou art.
To have thee is a thing made of gods' stuff
And to look on thee eternity's best part.

«But this is true and mine own art: the god
Thou art now is a body made by me,
For, if thou art now flesh reality
Beyond where men age and night cometh still,
'Tis to my love's great making power thou owest
That life thou on thy memory bestowest
And mak'st it carnal. Had my love not held
An empire of my mighty legioned will,
Thou to gods' consort hadst not been compelled.

«My love that found thee, when it found thee did
But find its own true body and exact look.
Therefore when now thy memory I bid
Become a god where gods are, I but move

To death's high column's top the shape it took
And set it there for vision of all love.

«O love, my love, put up with my strong will
Of loving to Olympus, be thou there
The latest god, whose honey-coloured hair
Takes divine eyes! As thou wert on earth, still
In heaven bodifully be and roam,
A prisoner of that happiness of home,
With elder gods, while I on earth do make
A statue for thy deathlessness' seen sake.

«Yet thy true deathless statue I shall build
Will be no stone thing, but that same regret
By which our love's eternity is willed.
One side of that is thou, as gods see thee
Now, and the other, here, thy memory.
My sorrow will make that men's god, and set
Thy naked memory on the parapet
That looks upon the seas of future times.
Some will say all our love was but our crimes;
Others against our names the knives will whet
Of their glad hate of beauty's beauty, and make
Our names a base of heap whereon to rake
The names of all our brothers with quick scorn.
Yet will our presence, like eternal Morn,
Ever return at Beauty's hour, and shine
Out of the East of Love, in light to enshrine
New gods to come, the lacking world to adorn.

«All that thou art now is thyself and I.
Our dual presence has its unity
In that perfection of body which my love
By loving it, became, and did from life
Raise into godness, calm above the strife
Of times, and changing passions far above.

«But since men see more with the eyes than soul,
Still I in stone shall utter this great dole;
Still, eager that men hunger by thy presence,
I shall to marble carry this regret
That in my heart like a great star is set.
Thus, even in stone, our love shall stand so great
In thy statue of us, like a god's fate,
Our love's incarnate and discarnate essence,
That, like a trumpet reaching over seas
And going from continent to continent,
Our love shall speak its joy and woe, death-blent,
Over infinities and eternities.

«And here, memory or statue, we shall stand,
Still the same one, as we were hand in hand
Nor felt each other's hand for feeling feeling.
Men still will see me when thy sense they take.
The entire gods might pass, in the vast wheeling
Of the globed ages. If but for thy sake,
That, being theirs, hadst gone with their gone band,
They would return, as they had slept to wake.

«Then the end of days when Jove were born again
And Ganymede again pour at his feast
Would see our dual soul from death released
And recreated unto joy, fear, pain —
All that love doth contain;
Life — all the beauty that doth make a lust
Of love's own true love, at the spell amazed;
And, if our very memory wore to dust,
By some gods' race of the end of ages must
Our dual unity again be raised.»

It rained still. But slow-treading night came in,
Closing the weary eyelids of each sense.
The very consciousness of self and soul
Grew, like a landscape through dim raining, dim.
The Emperor lay still, so still that now
He half forgot where now he lay, or whence
The sorrow that was still salt on his lips.
All had been something very far, a scroll
Rolled up. The things he felt were like the rim
That haloes round the moon when the night weeps.

His head was bowed into his arms, and they
On the low couch, foreign to his sense, lay.
His closed eyes seemed open to him, and seeing
The naked floor, dark, cold, sad and unmeaning.
His hurting breath was all his sense could know.
Out of the falling darkness the wind rose

And fell; a voice swooned in the courts below;
And the Emperor slept.
                              The gods came now
And bore something away, no sense knows how,
On unseen arms of power and repose.

Lisbon, 1915.

Bibliography

Pauly Ellen Bothe, *Apreciações Literárias de Fernando Pessoa* (Lisbon: Imprensa Nacional – Casa da Moeda, 2013).

Mariana Gray de Castro, *Fernando Pessoa's Shakespeare: The Invention of the Heteronyms* (London: Critical, Cultural and Communications Press, 2015).

Patricio Ferrari, Jerónimo Pizarro (eds), *Fernando Pessoa as English Reader and Writer* (Portuguese Literary and Cultural Studies, 28) (Dartmouth: Tagus Press at University of Massachusetts Dartmouth, 2015).

José Gil, *Fernando Pessoa ou la Métaphysique des Sensations* (Paris: Éditions de la Différence, 1988).

Hubert D. Jennings, *Fernando Pessoa: The Poet with Many Faces*, ed. Carlos Pitella (Lisbon: Tinta-da-China, 2019).

Teresa Rita Lopes, *Pessoa por Conhecer*, Vols I & II (Lisbon: Editorial Estampa, 1990).

———, (org.), *Pessoa inédito* (Lisbon: Livros Horizonte, 1993).

Fernando Cabral Martins (org.), *Dicionário de Fernando Pessoa e do Modernismo Português* (Lisbon: Editorial Caminho, 2008).

George Monteiro, *Fernando Pessoa and Nineteenth-Century Anglo-American Literature* (Kentucky: University Press of Kentucky, 2000).

George Monteiro, *The Presence of Pessoa: English, American, and South African Responses* (Kentucky: University Press of Kentucky, 1998).

Fernando Pessoa, *A Família Crosse*, Nuno Ribeiro & Cláudia Souza (eds) (Lisbon: Apenas Livros, 2019).

———, *A Língua Portuguesa*, ed. Luísa Medeiros (Lisbon: Assírio & Alvim, 1997).

———, *A Little Larger than the Entire Universe*, ed. and tr. by Richard Zenith (New York: Penguin Books, 2006).

———, *Antinous* (Lisbon: Monteiro & Co., 1918).

———, *Correspondência: 1923–1935*, ed. Manuela Parreira da Silva (Lisbon: Assírio & Alvim, 1999).

———, *Crítica — Artigos, Ensaios e Entrevistas*, ed. Fernando Cabral Martins (Lisbon: Assírio & Alvim, 2000).

———, *Crónicas da Vida que Passa*, ed. Pedro Sepúlveda (Lisbon: Ática, 2011).

———, *English Poems I–II* (Lisbon: Olisipo, 1921).

———, *Ensaio sobre Poesia*, ed. Nuno Ribeiro (Lisbon: Apenas Livros, 2020).

———, *Escritos Autobiográficos, Automáticos e de Reflexão Pessoal*, ed. Richard Zenith (Lisbon: Assírio & Alvim, 2003).

———, *Eu sou uma antologia: 136 autores fictícios*, Jerónimo Pizarro and Patricio Ferrari (eds) (Lisbon: Tinta-da-China: 2013).

———, *Heróstrato e a Busca da Imortalidade*, ed. Richard Zenith (Lisbon: Assírio & Alvim, 2000).

———, *O Regresso dos Deuses e Outros Escritos de António Mora* (Lisbon: Assírio & Alvim, 2013).

———, *Obra Completa de Álvaro de Campos*, Jerónimo Pizarro and Antonio Cardiello (eds) (Lisbon: Tinta-da-China, 2014).

———, *Obra Completa de Alberto Cæiro*, Jerónimo Pizarro and Patricio Ferrari (eds) (Lisbon: Tinta da China, 2016).

———, *Obras de António Mora*, ed. Luís Filipe B. Teixeira (Lisbon: Imprensa Nacional — Casa da Moeda, 2002).

————, *Páginas de Estética e de Teoria e Crítica Literárias*, Georg Rudolf Lind and Jacinto do Prado Coelho (eds) (Lisbon: Ática, 1966).

————, *Páginas Íntimas e de Auto-Interpretação*, Georg Rudolf Lind and Jacinto do Prado Coelho (eds) (Lisbon: Ática, 1966).

————, *Poemas Ingleses*, Tomo I, ed. João Dionísio (Lisbon: Imprensa Nacional — Casa da Moeda, 1993).

————, *Sensacionismo e Outros Ismos*, ed. Jerónimo Pizarro (Lisbon: Imprensa Nacional — Casa da Moeda, 2009).

————, *Teoria da Heteronímia*, Fernando Cabral Martins and Richard Zenith (eds) (Lisbon: Assírio & Alvim, 2012).

————, *Sobre a Arte Literária*, Fernando Cabral Martins and Richard Zenith (eds) (Lisbon: Assírio & Alvim, 2018).

————, *The Selected Prose of Fernando Pessoa*, ed. and translated by Richard Zenith (New York: Grove Press, 2001).

J.D. Reed, "Pessoa's Antinous," in *Pessoa Plural*: 10 (O./Fall 2016) 106–119.

Nuno Ribeiro, "Fernando Pessoa: The Plural Writing and the Sensationist Movement," in *Hyperion*, Vol. V, № 2 (November 2010) 73–95.

————, "Poéticas do Inacabado — Pessoa, Wittgenstein e o Livro por Vir," in: Osmar Pereira Oliva (org.), *Literatura, Vazio e Danação* (Montes Claros: Editora Unimontes, 2013) 223–241.

————, "Wittgenstein and Pessoa: The Archive as 'Open Work' in Eco's Perspective," in ARANCIBIA, Pamela Arancibia, J.L. Bertolio, Joanne Granata, Giovanna Licata, Erika Papagni, Matteo Ugolini, *Philological Concerns:*

Textual Criticism Throughout the Centuries (Firenze: Franco Cesati Editore, 2016) 207–221.

Nuno Ribeiro, Cláudia Souza (eds), *Fernando Pessoa & Walt Whitman* (Lisbon: Apenas Livros, 2018).

Arnaldo Saraiva, *Fernando Pessoa Poeta – Tradutor de Poetas* (Porto: Lello Editores, 1996).

Manuela Parreira da Silva, "Trochee, Prof.," In Fernando Cabral Martins (org.), *Dicionário de Fernando Pessoa e do Modernismo Português* (Lisbon: Editorial Caminho, 2008).

Pedro Sepúlveda, Jorge Uribe, "Planeamento editorial de uma obra em potência: o autor, crítico e tradutor Thomas Crosse," in: *Revista Colóquio / Letras*, № 183 (2013) 57–79.

Cláudia Souza, "Fernando Pessoa e a literatura inglesa," in *Revista da Anpoll*, Vol. I, № 36 (2014) 312–329.

———, *Fernando Pessoa e os Romantismos: Inglês, Francês, Português e Alemão* (Lisbon: Apenas Livros, 2019).

Richard Zenith, *Pessoa: An Experimental Life* (London: Penguin Books, 2021).

About the Editors

Nuno Ribeiro is a specialist in the Pessoa Archive and a postdoctoral fellow at IELT (Institute for the Study of Literature and Tradition) (FSCH, UNL), with a scholarship (SFRH/BPD/121514/2016) financed by FCT — Foundation for Science & Technology — under the FSE. He is the author of more than 20 books — editions and studies — about Fernando Pessoa's work published in Europe, Brazil, and the United States.

E-mail: nuno.f.ribeiro@sapo.pt

Cláudia Souza is a specialist in the Pessoa Archive and a researcher at CFUL Centre of Philosophy of the University of Lisbon. She is the author of more than 20 books — editions & studies — about Fernando Pessoa's work published in Europe, Brazil, and the United States.

E-mail: claudiasouzzza@hotmail.com

COLOPHON

WRITINGS ON ART & POETICAL THEORY
was handset in InDesign CC.

The text font is *Adobe Warnock*.
The display font is *KyivType Serif*.

Book design & typesetting: Alessandro Segalini
Cover design: Alessandro Segalini & CMP

Cover image: William Hogarth, *Characters and Caricaturas*
(April 1743), etching.

WRITINGS ON ART & POETICAL THEORY
is published by Contra Mundum Press.

Contra Mundum Press   New York · London · Melbourne

CONTRA MUNDUM PRESS

Dedicated to the value & the indispensable importance of the individual voice, to works that test the boundaries of thought & experience.

The primary aim of Contra Mundum is to publish translations of writers who in their use of form and style are *à rebours*, or who deviate significantly from more programmatic & spurious forms of experimentation. Such writing attests to the volatile nature of modernism. Our preference is for works that have not yet been translated into English, are out of print, or are poorly translated, for writers whose thinking & æsthetics are in opposition to timely or mainstream currents of thought, value systems, or moralities. We also reprint obscure and out-of-print works we consider significant but which have been forgotten, neglected, or overshadowed.

There are many works of fundamental significance to *Weltliteratur* (& *Weltkultur*) that still remain in relative oblivion, works that alter and disrupt standard circuits of thought — these warrant being encountered by the world at large. It is our aim to render them more visible.

For the complete list of forthcoming publications, please visit our website. To be added to our mailing list, send your name and email address to: info@contramundum.net

Contra Mundum Press
P.O. Box 1326
New York, NY 10276
USA

OTHER CONTRA MUNDUM PRESS TITLES

THE FUTURE OF KULCHUR
A PATRONAGE PROJECT

LEND CONTRA MUNDUM PRESS (CMP) YOUR SUPPORT

With bookstores and presses around the world struggling to survive, and many actually closing, we are forming this patronage project as a means for establishing a continuous & stable foundation to safeguard our longevity. Through this patronage project we would be able to remain free of having to rely upon government support &/or other official funding bodies, not to speak of their timelines & impositions. It would also free CMP from suffering the vagaries of the publishing industry, as well as the risk of submitting to commercial pressures in order to persist, thereby potentially compromising the integrity of our catalog.

CAN YOU SACRIFICE $10 A WEEK FOR KULCHUR?

For the equivalent of merely 2–3 coffees a week, you can help sustain CMP and contribute to the future of kulchur. To participate in our patronage program we are asking individuals to donate $500 per year, which amounts to $42/month, or $10/week. Larger donations are of course welcome and beneficial. All donations are tax-deductible through our fiscal sponsor Fractured Atlas. If preferred, donations can be made in two installments. We are seeking a minimum of 300 patrons per year and would like for them to commit to giving the above amount for a period of three years.